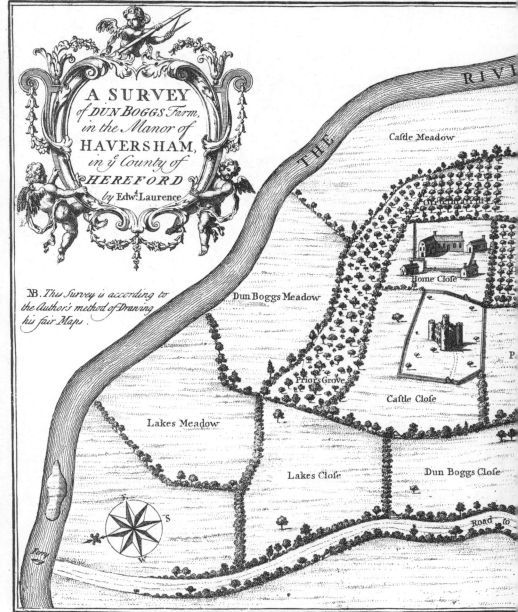

A SURVEY
of *DUN BOGGS* Farm,
in the *Manor* of
HAVERSHAM,
in ye *County* of
HEREFORD
by Edwd. Laurence

NB. *This Survey is according to*
the Author's method of Drawing
his fair Maps.

THE RIV[E]

Castle Meadow

Home Close

Dun Boggs Meadow

Priors Grove

Castle Close

Lakes Meadow

Lakes Close

Dun Boggs Close

Road to

S

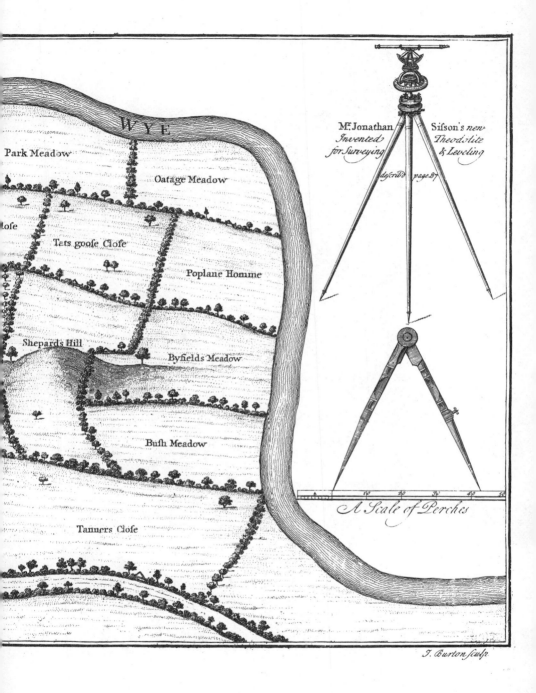

WYE

Park Meadow

Oatage Meadow

lose

Tats goose Close

Poplane Homme

Shepard's Hill

Byfields Meadow

Bush Meadow

Tanners Close

Mr. Jonathan Sifson's *new*
Invented *Theodolite*
for Surveying *& Leveling*

describ'd page 87

A Scale of Perches

10   20   30   40   50

J. Burton sculp.

THE
DUTY
OF
A Steward *to his* LORD,

Reprefented under

Several *Plain* and *Diftinct* ARTICLES; wherein may be feen the **Indirect Practices** of feveral S T E W A R D S, tending to **Leffen**, and the feveral **Methods** likely to **Improve** their LORDS Eftates.

To which is added an

APPENDIX,
SHEWING
The Way to Plenty,

Propofed to the F A R M E R S; wherein are laid down general *Rules* and *Directions* for the *Management* and *Improvement* of a FARM.

BOTH

Defign'd originally for the Ufe of the feveral *Stewards* and *Tenants* of His Grace the Duke of *Buckingham*, and NOW Improv'd and publifh'd for the general Ufe and Intereft of ALL the Nobility and Gentry throughout ENGLAND.

By E D W A R D L A U R E N C E, *Land-Surveyor.*

L O N D O N,

Printed for JOHN SHUCKBURGH, at the *Sun* between the two *Temple-Gates* in *Fleet-ftreet.* 1727.

ISBN 0 576 53202 9

Republished in 1971 by Gregg International Publishers Limited
Westmead, Farnborough, Hants., England
Printed in England.

To Her GRACE the

Dutchefs of *Buckingham-fhire* and *Normanby.*

Madam,

HE Remarks and Obferva-
tions relating to the Duty
and Office of a Steward,
which I here humbly offer
to Your Grace, are founded upon the Experience of *many* Years, and on fuch Reafo-
nings

nings as have had the Honour of *Your Grace*'s Approbation; upon both thefe accounts, I am perfuaded, they will be readily entertain'd by Perfons of the higheft Rank, who are chiefly concern'd in them; and by thofe more efpecially who have already fuffer'd thro' the *Knavery* and *Unfaithfulnefs* of their Stewards. And as it was for the fake of fuch that I undertook this Work, it is a peculiar fatisfaction to me, that I have the Honour of fending it into the World under the *Patronage* and *Protection* of a Perfon eminently diftinguifh'd for a *Superior* Judgment and *Good* Senfe; for an uncommon *Sagacity* in finding out the *T R U T H*, and an unweary'd application in the laying open and punifhing *F A L S H O O D*.

Were

Dedication.

Were I able to attempt the moſt imper-
fect Sketch of Your Grace's Character, I
ſhould mention that ſingular Candour and
Condeſcenſion, that eaſineſs of Acceſs to
Inferiors, which I have ſo often experienc'd,
and which ſo naturally attracts Love and
Admiration: I ſhou'd mention the Tryals
Your Grace has had of almoſt *every* Fortune,
and under *every* Relative Duty, in Life;
what *Prudence* in all of them; what *Firmneſs*
and *Courage* under the greateſt difficulties;
what *Humanity* and *Generoſity* have in their
turns preſided in your Life, and produc'd
the juſteſt Conduct under ſo various Cir-
cumſtances.

But

Dedication.

But I cannot omit what has fallen more fully under my Obfervation, and ought in Juftice to be taken notice of, That with an unufual Affiduity and Application to Bufinefs Your Grace has furmounted the greateft, and feemingly infuperable Difficulties, in the *preferving* and *retrieving* an Eftate ready to be *fwallow'd up in ruin*; not fo much by the Neglect, as the *Villany* of a fet of unjuft Stewards, who had made all manner of ill Ufes of the late Duke's *Abfence* from them.

A Defign truly worthy of a Parent's Care; which *few* Ladies with fuch an indefatigablenefs of Body and Mind cou'd have purfu'd and executed: *Few* wou'd have had

an

an Inclination to undertake; and this at a time when Your Grace was Miſtreſs of your own Actions, and in a ſeaſon of Life which might naturally have led you to paſs away the Hours in that proſperous Indolence and Eaſe you were left poſſeſs'd of.

That Your Grace may long Live, and have the Pleaſure of ſeeing the wiſe and noble Uſe the *Duke* of *Buckingham,* your Son, will make of all the Advantages you have procur'd him; That he may daily add to thoſe great Improvements, which he already promiſes, and which cannot fail of *flowing* from the Prudent Care you have taken, and continue to take, of *his Educa-*

tion ;

Dedication.

tion; as it is the greateſt ſatisfaction Your Grace propoſes in Life, ſo is it the moſt ſincere Wiſh of,

Madam,

Your Grace's

Moſt Dutiful, and

Moſt-Obedient Servant,

Edward Laurence.

THE

THE

PREFACE.

TH E *Misfortunes and Loſſes that have befallen ſeveral* of the Nobility *and* Gentry *throughout the King-dom, on account of either the* Ignorance *or* Knavery of bad Stewards, *will of themſelves be a* Sufficient Apology *for this Undertaking; even tho' the* Subject *it ſelf is* wholly new, *and the Attempt of finding out a* Remedy *for a ſpreading and unhappy* Diſeaſe *be difficult and dangerous.*

'T*is now above* Twenty Years *ſince I firſt began to apply my ſelf to* Survey Noblemens *and* Gentlemens Eſtates; *and at the ſame time to make the moſt* Exact Obſervations *about the different Methods of* Husbandry *and* Improvement, *where-ever I went. This naturally led we into an* Acquaintance *with* Stewards *and* Farmers; *and when I had made my ſelf a tolerable Maſter of*

(✻a)   *what*

The PREFACE.

what was both their Duty *and their* Interest *to pursue,* I *soon found room to Complain (within my self) of great, of very great,* Misfortunes *which* Lords *and* Gentlemen *too frequently lay under, from the* Ignorance *and* Slothfulness *of some, and the* Knavery *and* Wickedness *of others.*

The Consideration of these things, I *own, made so deep an Impression upon my* Mind, *that* I *quickly brought my self to these two following* Resolutions : First, *Not to engage my self in the* Office *and* Business *of a* Steward, *let the* Proposals *and* Offers *be never so* advantageous : *And, secondly, To publish to the World, some time or other, my* Thoughts *about the* Duty *of a* Steward, *chiefly with a* View *of correcting* Miscarriages, *and removing the Scandal which too often so* justly *attends the* Office.

The first of these Resolutions I *have hitherto preserv'd, under pretty strong and repeated* Temptations *from several Quarters to break it : And the second* I *am now performing, at a time when the whole* 𝖁𝖔𝖎𝖈𝖊 *of the* Kingdom *hath sounded with Indignation against a* 𝕱𝖔𝖗𝖌𝖊𝖗𝖞 *and consummate piece of* 𝖁𝖎𝖑𝖑𝖆𝖓𝖞 *in a* 𝕾𝖙𝖊𝖜𝖆𝖗𝖉, *grown immensely rich by a series of other* Unrighteous Designs *contriv'd against a* 𝕸𝖎𝖓𝖔𝖗 *and* Infant.

And altho' I *am not so vain as to think this short* Essay *will have any such abiding* Effect *upon the* Morals *of* Persons *concern'd, as quite to wear out the Disgrace usually attending the* Office, *or tempt me to break my first* Resolution ; *yet at least this pleasure and satisfaction* I *shall have in this Performance, that* I

shall

The PREFACE.

shall honeſtly *lay before the World what* I *have gather'd from* labour'd *Diligence and Obſervation, and what* I *take to be* right in the Office *and* Duty *of a* Steward, *with* reſpect *both to what he* ought, *and what he* ought *not to do.* And if in performing this I *uſe a Familiarity proper to make me* underſtood, I *hope it will not be imputed to me as a Fault, by thoſe of a politer* Taſte, *whilſt at the ſame time it may manifeſtly appear, that* I *aim to promote thoſe two* valuable *and* much-wanted *Things (the ſame in every place, and reſpected in every Age)* Truth and Ho-neſty.

In *directing the* Duty *and* Office *of a* 𝕾𝖙𝖊𝖜𝖆𝖗𝖉, I *found my ſelf alſo under a Neceſſity of ſaying* ſomething *to the* 𝕱𝖆𝖗𝖒𝖊𝖗, *whoſe Duty in many Caſes is pretty ſtrongly connected with that of the* Steward, *and without whoſe Diligence and Skill the* Steward *himſelf labours under* great Difficulties *and* unjuſt Reproofs. I *have therefore added an* APPENDIX, *wherein are laid down (gather'd from long Obſervation and diſtant Parts) ſuch* 𝖘𝖍𝖔𝖗𝖙 Rules *and* Directions *for the Management and Improvement of a* Farm, *as* I *purpoſe (* GOD *willing) ſome time or other* much *to enlarge upon.*

THE

THE
CONTENTS.

Introduction.

The

Articles relating to the Duty of a Steward.

Article I. *A* Steward *ſhould not undertake more Buſineſs than he can well perform, and a* Wrong *is done for want of regular Surveys; it being the leaſt part of the Buſineſs of a Steward to collect the Rents.* — — — — — — — — — Page 21

Art. II. *A Steward ought to be well vers'd in* Country-Buſineſs, *and in all the new Arts of* Improvement, *before he undertake that Office.* 22

Art. III. *The Steward's Buſineſs is to aſſign what Parcels of Lands are proper for* Paſture *and* Meadow, *and what others for* Tillage: *That the Tillage laid down for Graſs be re-enrich'd with proper Manure.*

23

Art.

Art.

Art.

The CONTENTS. xiii

AP-

A P P E N D I X.

— XII. *The*

Adver-

Advertisement.

Noblemens and Gentlemens Estates survey'd, in order to their Improvement; and Books of Maps, with the Particulars drawn from the said Surveys; shewing (under the proper Columns) the several sorts of Lands, whether *Arable, Pasture, Meadow*, or *Woodland*, in the possession of each Tenant.

By { *EDWARD LAURENCE,* Author of this Book.
A N D
WILLIAM GARDINER.

Who may be heard of at Mr. *Shucklurgh's*, a Bookseller; or at Mr. *Mead's*, a Goldsmith; both near *Temple-bar*; or at the Reverend Mr. *Laurence's*, at *Bishops-Weremouth* in the Bishoprick of Durham.

NB. The said Mr. Edward Laurence having had long Experience in *Country Business*, and the Nature of *Farms*; and having given full Satisfaction to a considerable part of the *Nobility* and *Gentry* by his own *Surveys*, which have enabled him first to *value*, and then to *let or sell* their Estates to the *best* Advantage; and likewise by drawing up *proper* Covenants to oblige their Tenants to keep up their Farms in a *due* Course of Husbandry: Gives Notice, That he is ready to serve the Nobility and Gentry farther, in Valuing and Letting their Estates, not only from his *Own Surveys*, but from those already done; and likewise gives Intelligence of *Estates* that are to be *Bought* and *Sold*.

ERRATA.

PAGE 11, Line 24, for *let* read *led*. Page 73, line ult. (under Column for the Value of the Head of each Tree) for 5 *l.* 6 *s.* 0 *d.* read 0 *l.* 5 *s.* 6 *d.* Page 93, in the Fig A B C D transpose B and C. Page 171, in the Column under 50, for 247.2 read 347.2. Page 176, in the Column under 64, for 1173.8 read 1137.8 Page 177, in the Column under 74, for 905.7 read 950.7

THE

THE
DUTY
OF

A Steward to his LORD, &c.

The Introduction.

THE following ARTICLES being sent into the World in a plain familiar Dress, and with a Freedom becoming an Artless HONESTY and *Simplicity*, I was willing, by way of *Introduction*, to advertise both *Nobleman* and *Steward* of some Particulars, which I conceive, may be of Use to *both*, and which I shall make use of with the same Ingenuous Freedom.

B   THAT

THAT the Art of *Husbandry* is of late Years greatly improv'd, is an undoubted Truth, confirm'd by every Day's Experience; and accordingly many Eftates have already admitted their *utmoft* Improvement; but much the greater number ftill remains of fuch as are fo far from being brought to that Perfection, that they have felt *few*, or *none*, of the Effects of Modern Arts and Experiments.

WHEN therefore a Lord of a Manor, either by his own Obfervation and Skill finds, or by the Advice and Experience of Others is made to underftand, that fuch Eftates, or fuch Parts of his Eftate, have been under a long Courfe of *bad* Government by *former Stewards*, or have otherwife fuffer'd by long Indolence and Neglect, altho' 'tis his great Wifdom to lofe no Time in entering upon a Reformation; yet he fhould not immediately think that *All* is to be fet right on a fudden; but Time and Patience muft be allow'd, and then Something may be done to Satisfaction : Nay, fomething more muft alfo be allow'd to recover and rectifie great Diforders; for if the Land hath been *pared* and *burnt*, or *over-plough'd* and *mow'd*, or otherwife impoverifh'd by felling the Hay and Straw off the Premifes; or if the Fences have gone to ruine, by the Carelefnefs of a Steward and Tenant; or if 'tis over-run with *Thorns*, *Whins*, and other Trumpery : In all, or any of thefe cafes, a Sum of Money *muft* be allow'd and expended to make good Deficiencies; and this, before the Landlord can, or ought fo much as to think of, any Advance of Rent : And therefore to anfwer his End moft effectually, and to do Things to the beft purpofe, a Refolution fhould be taken to keep fuch Farms in hand till they are a little reduc'd into Order; and after that, to let 'em to the beft Advantage. If fome fuch Method is not taken, I am pretty well affur'd, 'twill be very
diffi-

difficult to find Tenants that will anfwer either Rent or Expectation, except a *very long* Leafe be granted, to make the
Farms in fome meafure their own.

TENANTS in the *North*, who rent but fmall Farms, have,
generally fpeaking, but little Subftance wherewith to make
any expenfive Improvements. This indeed is a Misfortune, but 'tis fuch a one as requires Time to mend and
alter. To alter Farms, and to turn feveral little ones into
great ones, is a Work of Difficulty and Time ; for it would
raife too great an *Odium* to turn poor Families into the wide
World, by uniting Farms all at once, in order to make an
Advance of Rents : 'Tis much more reafonable and popular to be content to ftay till fuch Farms *fall* into Hand by
Death, before the Tenant is either rais'd or turn'd out. I
remember an Inftance, in my Surveys, of a Gentleman
who was for making fmall Farms into great ones all at
once, the Confequence whereof foon after appear'd to be
this ; That the *Church* and *Poor's* Seffes fell fo heavy upon
the remaining Tenants, that the Lord of the Manor was
foon brought to difcover his Miftake by re-admitting the
poor Tenants, and difpofing the Farms partly in the fame
ftate they were in before, and to content himfelf to allow
Time to compleat his Defire of *improving his Eftate* in *that*
Way of making the Farms larger.

THE true Remedy therefore for this Misfortune is not
the *violent* one of *forcing* them beyond their Power, but the
gentle and *rational* one of *perfuading*, and *inftructing* them in
all the thriving *Arts* of making the beft of their Farms,
that they may be able, not only to *pay*, but to *advance*
their Rents. I have known feveral Inftances of Tenants
that held their Lands at an Eafie *Old* Rent, and yet, for
want

want of being inftructed in the New Methods of *Lime*, *Turneps*, *Grafs-Seeds*, &c. were ftill poor, and hardly able to pay that *Old* Rent, much lefs could they bear any Advance : But yet, as foon as they became better inftructed by the Steward to practife all the beft and lateft Methods of Husbandry, they prefently could bear an Advance of Rent ; and not only *fuffer'd* it, but grew *richer* upon it, and *thriv'd* better than they did before at the *Old* Rent.

But forafmuch as it will appear, by what follows, that the Steward, if he acts as an *Honeft* Steward ought to act, will have always his Hands and his Head full of Bufinefs of many kinds, fo that he may be well excus'd the Trouble of being a conftant Inftructor to the Tenants ; and forafmuch as it is highly convenient to have a living Inftructor amongft many ignorant Farmers, to teach them, if poffible, both by Example and Precept, the readieft Way to *improve* their Farms, and to *enrich* themfelves, I would advife all Noblemen, and others, who cannot be at hand themfelves to fet forward Improvements, to get one or two Tenants out of the *South* and moft improv'd Countries, to fhew others the Way by their Example. And if it fhall be thought difficult to get Tenants to remove into a ftrange Country, a proper Perfon fhould be *hired*, who underftands the New Methods of preparing the Ground, and fent over, as well to manage a Farm in hand for his Lord, as to direct and inftruct others, till they fee with their own Eyes how much better *the Land gives her Encreafe*, order'd and manag'd with Wifdom and Skill.

I can-

I cannot forbear here to take notice, that Noblemen and Gentlemen lie under great Evils and Inconveniencies, when they suffer themselves to be persuaded to employ *Country Attorneys* for their Stewards ; because *it* seldom happens that they are well Qualified for that Trust. And indeed, if the Office of a Steward be any whit rightly describ'd in the following Articles, and his DUTY fairly explain'd, it may at one View be easily discern'd, that this Caution is well founded. A Steward's Business is not such as may be done as it were *by the by* : 'Tis his *whole* Employment, and a full one too ; and therefore he must *hoc agere.* The Attorney, if he has any Character, has Business enough of his own, of the Law, and therefore should not undertake the Office of a Steward, which, in most Parts of it, he doth not understand ; neither will his Employment let him : But I would always have the Steward consult the Attorney in matters relating to the Law, and to attend him at his *Court-keeping.*

I have known Instances where a Country Attorney has been Steward to seven or eight Noblemen, and others, and yet has done nothing else but attend the Court-keeping and collecting of Rents ; by which means the Tenants have taken the Advantage of doing what they would with their Farms, quickly lessening the Value of the Estates by *Over-ploughing,* &c. I have also observ'd on my Surveys, that these sort of indolent Stewards are commonly against the having their Lord's Estates survey'd and mapt, for fear of opening a *New Scene* : And yet their very warmness against *Surveys* and *Improvements* (calling the one *unnecessary,* and the other *unpopular*) has been the Occasion of putting all *Oeconomists* upon them.

FROM thefe, compar'd with the following reafons in the Articles, it will appear, what a great Truft a Steward has repos'd in him; and how much it is in his power to *Improve*, or make *worfe*, his Lord's Eftate. For which reafon it behoves every Landlord to ufe his utmoft Caution and Wifdom in the Choice of a Man of HONESTY and UNDERSTANDING for a Steward: However, I fee no reafon why he fhould not be under Covenants, and give fecurity to perform them, as well as the Tenants.

WHETHER the Hints I have here given, and fhall hereafter have Occafion to give, with refpect to *indirect practices* in many Stewards, be not well founded, I muft leave to Others to judge, who have had a *feeling* and thorow Senfe of that Matter: But I cannot forbear to take Notice of a particular pleafant Incidence in my Travels, which (becaufe I was my felf no Sufferer, nor had any hand in the fuffering of Others) hath often made me fmile.

" As I was, fome time fince, employ'd in *Surveying*
" and *Valuing* a Lord's Eftate in the *North*, Curiofity
" led the Nobleman himfelf to go along with me one
" Day, to look about him, to fee how his Eftate lay,
" and to view the Extent and Beauty of it. But before
" we enter'd upon Bufinefs, the *Steward* led us the way
" into his Compting-houfe, or (as he rather chofe to call
" it) his *Oratory*, or Place of Devotion; where he pre-
" fently fhew'd us (as lying at his Right-Hand) *South's*
" and *Waterland's* Sermons againft the growing HERESIES
" of this Age; Which Sermons (faith he, with Eyes lift
" up, and a devout Countenance) I read to my Family
" every *Sunday* Night, left they alfo be tempted to *deny*
" the

" *the Lord that bought them.* And thus, by ordering the
" matter fo, as to appear to his Lord at other times
" with a *Friday-Face* for every Day in the Week, he an-
" ticipated all fufpicion of *Knavery* or Wrong; infomuch
" that fometimes, with a fingular Pleafure, he would ex-
" prefs to me, *how happy he was in a Steward, that had fo*
" *good and orthodox a Senfe of Religion!* But, alas! before
" the Lord left the Country, he was told, to his forrow,
" that *The Zeal of his Houfe had even eaten him up :* For,
" upon a ftrict Enquiry into his Affairs, the Lord was
" quickly made to underftand, that this godly Steward
" had bought no lefs than Six hundred Pounds a Year un-
" der his very Nofe, which he purchas'd by being Steward
" only Fifteen Years; and, by all Accounts, he was not
" worth Ten Pounds when he enter'd. And the method
" by which he acquir'd thefe Riches is no lefs remarka-
" ble; for it was by receiving of the Tenants what he was
" pleas'd to call *Income-money*; telling them, It was an
" ancient *Perquifite* of a Steward : That is to fay, every
" year when he enter'd the Tenant's name anew into
" his Book, he receiv'd a B R I B E, for letting them hold
" their Farms at a *low Old Rent*, inftead of an *Improv'd one.*
" This was only One Part of his *unjuft Gain*; for he like-
" wife, on pecuniary Confiderations, fuffer'd the Tenants
" to ftock fome of the beft Land with Rabbits, conniv'd
" at their ploughing the beft Paftures and Meadows, and
" confented to the *paring,* and *burning,* and *fowing Rape*
" upon the beft Land, the *vile* and *beggaring* Effects
" whereof I have fully fhewn in the following ARTI-
" CLES.

MORE-

MOREOVER, it may not be amiſs to take Notice here, that whenever a Steward engageth himſelf in the Buſineſs of Farming on his own Account, it commonly proves a Loſs and a diſappointment to his Lord; becauſe that Buſineſs, if it is minded, (and he ſeldom will forget or neglect his own) takes up ſo great a part of his Time, that ſome neceſſary Article of Duty muſt be neglected; and it will be impoſſible for him to be upon the watch, as he ought, to ſee that the Tenants perform their Covenants.   It is alſo no leſs a diſadvantage to a Lord, when his Steward (and ſuch a caſe I have known) turns *Merchant*, by trading in *Corn, Malt, Butter, Cheeſe,* &c. the Product of the Eſtate; for, to my certain Knowledge, this Practice hath apparently prov'd a great leſſening of the Tenant's profit, whilſt by the *Authority* of the ſaid Steward the Tenant is frequently oblig'd, not only to pay his Rent in ſuch Commodities before 'tis due, but alſo at the Steward's own price, and at under-rates.   They held indeed their Farms at an *eaſie Old Rent*, but if the Steward, by theſe *knaviſh* indirect Practices, raiſes an Eſtate, it is plain *the Lord pays for it.* And yet, when theſe *vile* practices were put a Stop to, and the Tenants were advanc'd above a third Part, I have been aſſur'd, by the Tenant's own Confeſſion, that they got more money off their Farms, after their Rents were rais'd, than they did before.

IT is therefore, on all Accounts, much the *Wiſdom* and *Intereſt* of all Noblemen, and others, to allow their Stewards a *handſome Salary*, that they may be able, without new-invented *Perquiſites*, to live with reputation and Credit; by which they will preſerve an Authority over
the

the Tenants to keep Bufinefs in order. And if this is not done, the falfe *Oeconomy* of it will foon be paid dear for, in all the artful ways of *fqueezing* and *pinching* both Landlord and Tenant; as may appear by what hath been faid above.

As Prudence and Difcretion fhould govern every thing, fo, in following the Example of Others, great regard is to be had to them. In my Surveys I have met with Inftances of private Gentlemen of fmall Eftates living upon the fpot, who, led perhaps by neceffity or avarice, did *rack* their Tenants higher than the Land, by the moft laborious Induftry, could make any profitable Return; as hath appear'd by their conftant change of Tenants almoft every two or three years: But if Stewards acting for Perfons of Quality at a diftance, fhould be fo *rigid*, fhall I fay, or *imprudent*, as to practife this method, they would foon make their Lord, as well as themfelves, very uneafie by the *uncertainty* of the Rentals, by conftant *Arrears*, and by having the Lands often thrown into hand: But the greateft difadvantage of all is, the running a *hazard* of having the Eftate *beggar'd* and *impoverifh'd*. For, if Tenants are not at fome *Certainty*, they will be greatly difcourag'd from being good Husbands; at leaft, from laying out money whereby to *improve* their Farms. So that when a Steward is once fatisfied and convinc'd he hath let a Farm to an *honeft* advantage, his beft way then is, to let a Leafe for 15 or 21 years, at the fame time taking care to infert *proper Covenants*, fuch as in *this Treatife* he will be fufficiently inftructed in.

D

BUT

BUT I would not have it be fo underftood, as if I thought the fame Leafe and Rent were to be a ftanding Rule for *ever*. On the contrary it is certain, that the *Value* of Money every day and year *fluctuates*, and, in the general, hath been continually decreafing; and therefore the Rent of an Eftate in reafon ought to be adjufted to that Rule, and to be rais'd accordingly in proportion. Thefe (and the like) Arguments I have ufed with Tenants occafionally, as I found they would hear reafon. I told them, it was unreafonable to expect to rent a Farm *now*, when a fat Goofe is fold for *Two Shillings*, at the fame rate as *formerly*, when the fame Goofe was fold for a *Groat*. This familiar way of talking to them, I often found, made an impreffion on them with fuccefs, when other more refolute and rougher methods fail'd. In treating with Tenants they fhould be talk'd with in their own Language, and by Arguments which they throughly underftand, and have a feeling fenfe of. So that if a Steward would gain his point, he muft not hope to do it in the *bluftering* manner and method of fome Agents, whom I have known fent down from *London* in order to make an *Advance* of Rents, who yet know little or nothing of *Country Bufinefs*. One of thefe Agents, I remember, came down fully bent with a refolution to advance his Lord's Tenants *Six fhillings* in the pound one with another; and told them in a haughty fhort manner, they muft *turn out* if they did not comply. Thofe who rented *fmall* Farms, and were themfelves *poor*, was forced to fubmit, knowing not what to do, nor where to go; but the more difcerning and fubftantial Farmers, finding the Agent to talk more knowingly about *Affemblies* and *Ladies*, and underftood *Dreffing* better than Farming, foon defpis'd him, as ignorant of their Affairs,

and

and would not fubmit ; and fo he was forced to return to *London* juft as wife as he came down, without having done any bufinefs to the purpofe ; for, indeed, he might have ufed the fame *ridiculous* method of raifing the Rents by *poundage*, and have ftay'd at home.

WHEREAS had this Eftate been prudently manag'd by a Steward well vers'd in *Country Bufinefs*, and the beft methods of Husbandry ; had he had by him an accurate * Survey of the number of Acres of the feveral parcels of Lands, whether *arable*, *pafture*, or *meadow*, in the poffeffion of each Tenant ; and had he throughly underftood which Farms would admit of *moft*, and which of the *leaft* Improvements, he might eafily have fettled each Tenants Farm in a due *proportion* of Rent to their fatisfaction, without going in the fummary and *unjuft* way of *Poundage*. I call it *unjuft*, becaufe it falls heavy upon *fome*, and perhaps light on *others*. And indeed it is not feldom that I have known a Steward (to fhew a pretended diligence) has rais'd fome of the *fmall* Farms, that did not bring *Grift to his Mill*, and let the more *fubftantial* ones, who were able, go free and unrais'd, for reafons not to be named.

IF then Perfons of Quality will fuffer themfelves to be let into this method of advancing their Eftates by *poundage*, it may eafily be imagin'd what forrows and curfes they will draw upon themfelves, and what fad undefirable work will be made amongft the fmall Farms, when it fhall be once underftood, that they have been rais'd already.

IF

---

* See the Survey at the end of the Articles.

IF it will not be thought too much anticipating what is to follow in the *Articles*, I would here obferve, that a Steward who is mafter of Country-affairs, and hath made himfelf acquainted with *every* parcel of Land in each Tenant's poffeffion, when he comes to treat with a Tenant, in order to fettle a Rent equal to the Value of the Farm, fhould take his *Pen* in hand, and make a *Calculation* with the Tenant, how many *Head* of Cattel his Pafture will keep, according to its goodnefs; as alfo how many *Quarters* of the feveral forts of Grain his arable Land will produce one year with another, which may be judg'd of *nearly* by feeing the Crops in the feveral years: And again, how many *Loads* of Hay may be expected from the Meadows. From thefe, and fuch other D A T A'S, he may finifh a calculation of what may be fold off the Farm, which ought to be (as I fhall have further occafion hereafter to obferve) at leaft *two Rents*, if it is intended a Farmer fhould thrive; and *thrive he muft*, or elfe the Landlord will fuffer *firft* or *laft*. By thefe methods and fair *Calculations* a Farmer is treated in a familiar eafie way, and you beat, or rather *convict*, him with his own Weapons. But he will not be *bully'd* or *hector'd* into an advanc d Rent by thofe who know no reafon for what they do and fay: Whereas, by ufing him with Refpect and Civility, and appealing to his own Judgment and Experience, you bring him to Reafon and Conviction; you make a conqueft by talking in his own way, and fo *honourably* gain your point.

I muft confefs, I have fometimes met with fuch as would not be perfwaded or beat out of their own way of thinking, and therefore would hear *no* Reafons: In fuch cafe a Steward, before he begins to make an Advance

upon

upon an *old-rented Eftate*, fhould have an *over-rack'd* Tenant or two in his eye ready to put in, if any of the principal Tenants refuse, after a fair *Calculation* of the value of their Farms hath been made to them. This method I always found to have a good effect, and was a means of breaking the neck of a *Confederacy* or *Combination*, which fometimes will be obferv'd among the Tenants, when they agree together to make *no Advance.* The firft Example of a Tenant that will not liften to Reafon or civil treatment, fhould be us'd in fome fuch manner as followeth : Get it under his own Hand, that he *voluntarily* leaves his Farm on the Terms offer'd, *viz.* Thus :

Sept. 20. 1722.

I *Do bereby declare, that I have voluntarily left the Farm which I lately rented of his Grace the Duke of* K——; *and, that I freely confent that the fame fhould be rented by any other Perfon that offers, intending to leave the fame at* L. *Day next.*

Witnefs my Hand,

A. B.

I almoft always found, that when fuch a Certificate as this was offer'd to be fign'd, the Tenant (ftubborn as he was before) *boggled* at it, as thinking that *now* in earneft

E   neft

neft he muſt leave his Farm, if he ſets his Hand : Inſomuch that he commonly choſe to *conſider* of it, and to
have Time to ask his Wife leave, and to have her Con-
ſent : The conſequence of which was, that he ſeldom
fail'd to come again in a few days, and without more
ado, to ſtrike up a *bargain.* But if it ſo happen'd that
the Tenant was unperſwadable, and *would* ſign the aforeſaid Certificate, yet this method was of ſingular uſe in
procuring a *new* Tenant. They commonly make a ſort
of Conſcience of taking a Farm over another's head, as
they call it ; tho', it may be, an abſolute Refuſal has
been given ; and ſo, for want of ſome ſuch Teſtimony
under Hand, that *Shyneſs* would ſtill remain ; but, upon
producing it, all difficulties vaniſh'd, and *new* Tenants
readily enter'd into Articles.

THIS method had alſo another good effect ; for it put
a ſtop to all further Combinations, and, as it were, *Re-
bellions* againſt their Lord, uſually carried on in a *ſtupid,*
tho' a ſort of *ſacred* manner : For it is uſual with them
to aſſemble together round a *great Stone,* upon which
they are to SPIT, believing this Practice (joyn'd with
a Promiſe of what they will do, and ſtand to) to be as
ſacred and binding as if they had taken a publick *Oath.*
In this contrivance I will not ſuppoſe that they can prevail upon the *Vicar* of the place to *preach* againſt Improvements ; but if they can prevail upon the *Clark* of
the Pariſh (as ſometimes they have done) to ſet an
appoſite *Pſalm,* and make the Congregation *ſneer,* they applaud themſelves for their *Wit,* and conclude their buſineſs done.

                                                        I am

I am forry to fay thefe fort of mean contrivances have fometimes been not a little encourag'd underhand, by the Envy of fome of the Gentlemen of leffer Eftates, who, tho' they themfelves *ftretch* their Tenants Rents to the utmoft, yet hate that a Perfon of Quality, living in the *South*, fhould by his Steward fet up for *Oeconomy* and *Management*, fometimes not fparing even terms of reproach and popular fcandal, in order to caufe a *mutiny* among the Tenants : Which misfortune cannot otherwife be better and more effectually remedied, than by proper and occafional Refidence, whereby great Men (as I fhall have occafion in the Articles to obferve) endear themfelves to their Country, and thereby prevent the *Odium* which ufually attends the making any advancement in Rents ; whilft it appears that they do not carry away all their money and treafure, but are willing to fpend fome of it amongft them, by encouraging *Trade*, and by *Acts* of *Charity*.

I am unwilling to detain the Reader too long from the fubftance of my defign, or to tire him with too many Particulars in an Introduction ; but yet there are two Heads ftill remaining, which when explain'd, I fhould think, cannot fail to be acceptable to the Publick. And I fhall lay down what I have to fay by way of addrefs, (1.) to all *Noblemen*, and others, for the *choice* and *management* of their Stewards : And (2.) to the *legiflative powers*, that they would interpofe, to prevent the Abufes and mifchiefs occafion'd by common WATER-MILLS.

THE firft Head leads me to mention a fingular good method, taken by a Perfon of Quality, for the government and choice of his Stewards, as an Example to others. This good *Oeconomift*, whenever he comes down into the

Coun-

Country, (*and come they muſt, if they will have their Eſtates to thrive*) in looking into his Affairs, and the diſpoſition of his Eſtate, ever took care to have *all* his Agents and Stewards along with him, that they might *all* be acquainted with one another's Buſineſs, by knowing the ſeveral Tenants methods of managing their Farms, and alſo the true Value of them, that in caſe of Mortality or Removes, there might be no difficulty of a Steward's being a Stranger to any part of the whole Eſtate. And to carry this rational management a little further, I ſhould think it very proper, after a Steward hath liv'd five or ſix years upon one Eſtate, that he be mov'd to live five or ſix years upon another; and ſo to continue moving the whole Sett of them round, as the Noble-man or Gentleman ſees occaſion: The reaſon of which is very plain and diſcernible, *viz.* that hereby they will of conſequence prove a *checque* upon one another.

MOREOVER, that Perſons of Quality may never be at a loſs (in caſes of Mortality and Removes) to have a pro-per Steward to ſupply a *Vacancy*, it is very adviſeable and neceſſary to have always one, or more, of the Farmer's Sons in their eye, who are deem'd to be of a ſuitable Genius, and whoſe Education hath been ſuch, that they may be ſuppos'd not only to be expert in *Country-affairs*, but to bear the Character of ſupporting and purſuing TRUTH and HONESTY. When once the Lord is pretty well aſſur'd of this, 'twould very much contribute to the End in view, if a Preſent of Ten or Fifteen Guineas apiece was made to the Parents, to have them well inſtructed in *Accompts*, &c. and to let fall ſomething that may *encourage* their Hopes of being provided for in a better manner than can reaſonably be expected from moſt Trades and Profeſſions, which are ob-ſerv'd of late Years to be ſo generally overſtock'd, that

more

more than half of the Profeffors throughout the Kingdom are driven to neceffities and ftraits. When fome fuch methods as thefe are taken, whereby the brighter part of the Country Youth are made to hope for *preferment* in their Lord's fervice, or to be recommended to others upon occafion, it may eafily be concluded, that no fmall Advantage muft accrue towards the *Improvement* of Eftates in general, from a *Nurfery* and (as it were) *Seminary* of young men inftructed, as they ought to be, in all the HONEST *Arts of good Husbandry and good Accompts.*

POSSIBLY the Freedom I have taken, and the Plainnefs I have us'd, may be thought by fome to need an Apology, becaufe fome of the *Articles* at firft view may by *Stewards* be interpreted as *Ill-nature* in me, as if I had had a *prejudice* to, or *fet my felf* againft them in general; but, alas! I have neither *Intereft* nor *Inclination* to ferve in being ill-natur'd or fatyrical: I would difcourage and detect *Knavery*, and I would do all I can to convince Stewards that *Honefty* and *Truth* are the beft Policy. Stewards indeed are, of all others, under the greateft temptation to be Knaves, becaufe they have it fo much in their power to be fuch, with impunity, and without difcovery: They are born like other men, and have not more Corruptions in their nature; and, were I to give Inftances, I could name many who are *above* all the little *Arts* of *robbing* their Lord to *enrich* themfelves: And if there are others not true to their Truft, their Faults fhould be writ in their *Foreheads*; and I am not afham'd to fay, *I have done, and will do* all I can to make them known, and to prevent indirect Practices for the future.

F   MORE-

MOREOVER, if it be ftill objected and ask'd, (as I forefee fome may ask) *Who would be a Lord's Steward, if they muft have fo many Eyes and fo many Checques upon them?* let fuch confider, that *Lofers* and the *Cheated* have not only a right to complain, but alfo to contrive the beft methods to fecure and defend themfelves from future *Injuries*. Neither can I think that an *honeft* and *wife* Steward will have any reafon to diflike thefe methods ; and as for thofe that are otherwife, the world is generally juft and equitable enough not to regard their Complaints.

To conclude this Head ; I cannot however avoid faying, that it is the Intereft, and fhould be the Refolution, of every Nobleman, when he is perfwaded he hath a *faithful* Steward, to ftudy to make him as eafie as poffible by all fitting *Encouragements*, and not to *liften* to or entertain every *officious* Story that will be told, except there be very good grounds ; much lefs to difcharge him on the account of *fufpicion* only. To do that (*and yet that is too often done*) were the fure way never to be ferv'd with *Truth* and *Honefty* : For it may be a temptation to fome Stewards, when they find their Office is precarious, to make the beft they can of it in a *little* time, by ways not altogether *juftifiable* ; *Encouragement* goes a great way towards putting *evil* thoughts out of their minds. I remember an Inftance of the *generofity* of a certain Lord, that when his Steward had balanc'd a faithful Account, and had obferv'd that the Eftate was *improv'd*, would make him a handfome Prefent, befides the allowance of his fettled Salary.

MUCH the fame may be faid with refpect to Tenants ; if they are bound down to hard Meafures and Articles regarding only the Intereft of the Lord, they will have

no

no Encouragement to *improve* their Farms, but on the contrary will be tempted to contrive ways to *evade* the force of their Leafes to fupply Deficiencies, efpecially as they are near *expiring*, attended with fuch Expoftulations as thefe : *What Encouragement have we to improve , if we muft pay for it when our Leafes are out, upon that* very *account ?*

THE fecond Head leads me to an Addrefs to the LEGISLATIVE POWERS, that they would interpofe (for the Good of the Publick, and their own fakes) to prevent the Abufes and Mifchiefs occafion'd by WATER-MILLS. For it is well known, that moft of the loweft Meadows and beft Lands in *England* are more or lefs affected and hurt by Water-mills, which fometimes wholly prevent the draining and drawing off fuch ftagnating Waters, as tend to fpoil the very *beft Land* ; and at other times prevent the great advantages which the Meadows near Rivers might receive by being *flooded* with *Frefhes* and *White-water*. In fhort, they caufe the overflowings of large and brave Eftates, to their *utter Ruine* ; and they prevent the Improvements which might be made upon others ; to fay nothing here of the dead weight which they ever prove upon the good Defigns of making Rivers *navigable*.

ALL which Abufes, I am well affur'd from a Perfon of undeniable Judgment and Skill in fuch affairs, may be perfectly remedied, and the neceffary bufinefs of grinding Corn, *&c.* as effectually perform'd, as ever was in the common methods.

THE

THE Commiſſioners of *Sewers* have little Encouragement to take pains and perform their duty, whilſt they conſtantly find their Deſigns prove abortive, on account of the preſent ſcituation of *Water-mills*, the ſettling of which Inconveniencies I refer to the conſideration of Perſons in Power, and others, whoſe Eſtates are hurt thereby.

The

Article I.

I Begin with a MAXIM which is highly to be regarded, *viz.* That a Steward undertake not more buſineſs than he can truly and regularly and *honeſtly* perform. And this Caution is to be underſtood, not only of ſuch *variety* of Buſineſs and Affairs of different Kinds, as tend to diſtract the head, but even of a *multiplicity* of proper buſineſs relating to a Steward ; eſpecially if that Buſineſs happen to lie in many and diſtant parts : For (as it will appear in the following *Articles*) it is the leaſt part of the Buſineſs of a Steward to collect the Rents ; and he may as effectually wrong his Lord for want of proper and *regular* Surveys, as for a neglect in gathering his rents.

G

Article

Article **II.**

NO one fhould undertake the Bufinefs of a Steward till he is fully acquainted with Country Affairs, fo as to be able, upon *all* occafions, to direct and advife fuch Tenants as do not underftand the *beft* and *lateft* Improvements in Husbandry. And this Knowledge is the more neceffary, becaufe fometimes a Farm ill manag'd by a former Tenant, happens to fall into the Lord's hand ; and then a regular and Experienc'd Skill in the Steward will be very feafonable, as well as of great fervice to his Lord, by fhewing an *Example* of good Husbandry to the reft of the Tenants.

Article **III.**

A Steward fhould, at the *firft* entring into his Service, make himfelf mafter of the Quantity and Quality of *every* parcel of Land occupied by the feveral Tenants ; and this will enable him to confider and advife what Parcels are proper to be kept for *Pafture* and *Meadow*, and. what

what other parcels for *Tillage*: An Example whereof is drawn out from an accurate Survey at the end of this Trea-tife *. But it fhould be added here, that great Care ought to be taken that *none* of the Tenants be allow'd to have much above a third part of the Farm in Tillage in any one year, (except 'tis fuch poor Land as is fubject to be over-run with Trumpery for want of ploughing) obliging them alfo to lay the fame down, after a reafonable term of years, with proper † Grafs-feeds; *viz.* after about four Crops taken, and two Summer Fallows given. And the fame Care fhould be had, that the Lands, when laid down, be fupply'd and re-enrich'd with a proper quan-tity of Manure; Twenty Loads of Dung fuppofe upon an Acre, or Ninety Bufhels of Lime. A confiderable ftrefs fhould be laid upon the due performance of this Article; becaufe, from *long* Experience and *repeated* Ob-fervation, it hath *ever* appear'd to me, that the laying down Lands *poor*, without proper Supplies, hath been the *Ruine of many Farms*, and put a ftop to *all* fuch reafonable Advance of rent as might have been made, by rendering it almoft impoffible (without an *immenfe* Charge) to reftore its former *riches* and *ftrength*.

---

* See the Survey.   † See the Appendix.

Arti-

Article IV.

A Steward fhould endeavour to make himfelf mafter of the *Method* that every Tenant takes, to raife his Lord's Rent, as well as to provide for his Family : And if he finds a Tenant, either thro' Ignorance or Indolence, not likely to thrive, or does not proceed in a due courfe of Husbandry, that then he firft *admonifh* and *inftruct* him ; and, if he proves *ftubborn* and *unperfwadable*, afterwards to *difcharge* him, and put another in his room, before he run too far *behindhand* in his Rents, which is a fure Fore-runner of an irretrievable Poverty, and a too fevere tryal of a good-natur'd Landlord. To prevent therefore the worft Extremity, and that thefe and the following *Articles* may be moft effectually perform'd, *a Steward fhould ride over the whole Eftate at leaft once a month*, in order to view both the Lands and Stock of the Tenants carefully and diftinctly, taking MEMORANDUMS of the fame from time to time ; which will prove no fmall *cheque* upon the feveral Tenants, and will be of confiderable advantage to both *Landlord* and *Tenant*.

Arti-

Article V.

A Steward, on his Survey round his Lord's Eftate, fhould be careful to obferve that the Tenants do not plough up any frefh Pafture or Meadow Ground, without firft giving notice to the Lord of the Manor, or fuch Agents as he fhall appoint. According to the beft of my Obfervation and Judgment, I could never find but that it is the *Intereft* of every *Landlord* to fuffer the Tenant to grub up *Whins, Thorns,* and *Broom,* that have over-run fome of the *worfer* fort of Land, and then to ufe it for Four or Six Years in *Tillage,* without any expectation of advance of rent, provided the fame be laid down with ✶ Grafs-Seeds (of which more hereafter) and a proper quantity of Dung. But if the Land be of the better fort, and (which is frequently the cafe) by age fubject to grow over with Mofs ; in fuch cafe, altho' it is of real advantage to the Land to turn it up with the Plough, yet a confiderable † Encreafe of Rent ought to be made for the *Advantage* of ploughing fuch *frefh* Ground, for three years only : And the Tenant fhould be oblig'd to lay down the fame with about Twenty Loads of Dung, or Ninety Bufhels of Lime, upon an Acre, according to the nature of the Land, which is fully fhewn in the Appendix.

✶ See the Appendix.   † See Stewards Accompts.

Article VI.

A Steward, on his Surveys, fhould ftrictly obferve and order, that the Lord's Tenants, as well as thofe of the Freeholder's, do conftantly from time to time, as need requires, cleanfe and fcowr up their Ditches, in order to carry off the Water into the *Vales*, *Rivers*, or *Sewers*, if any fuch there be, within the faid Manors. For which purpofe it is requifite that the Steward be always oblig'd to attend the COURT-LEET and COURT-BARON, in order to PRESENT fuch Tenants as have been guilty of Neglects in the aforemention'd Particulars, that they may be *fined* according to Law. The force of this Article, in making Stewards the Agents in this Affair, lieth here : That it is known by Experience and Obfervation, if they are not *prefented* by the Steward, the Tenants will not *prefent* one another ; which occafions great Delays and Difappoint-ments, to the manifeft damage of Eftates. It is alfo very proper that a Steward fhould be qualified to be one of the Commiffioners of *Sewers*, that he may be an Inftru-ment always at hand to pufh forward the performance of this Article, and the executing the commendable Husban-dry of fcowring and cleanfing the feveral Ditches and Trenches, which otherwife would foon become of little or no ufe.

N.B. For

N. B. For the better direction of a Steward, it may not be amiss in this place to mention an excellent part of good Husbandry much practis'd in the *West* of *England*, where they plough Trenches about two foot deep with a Plough made on purpose with a double Coulter: After that they dig the said trenches till they are full four foot deep, and considerably wider at the top than at the bottom, into which they cast all the green brush-wood of *Black-thorns, Withies, White-thorns,* &c. which they can muster up together, laying flat Stones upon them, to keep them tight together; and then the Drain is finish'd by filling the trenches up with the rubbish plough'd and dug out of them. This method teaches the Farmer the advantage of having his over-moist ground always dry; and, for the future, he will have the profit of losing no part of the Herbage. Again,

I hope it will not be thought too great a digression, if for the Steward's direction and information, I here transcribe Mr. *Switzer's* recommended method of draining Land by artificial Tubes or Trunks of Clay, which, he saith, hath prov'd one of the most useful Inventions that has been found out in any Age, and will do in *pasture, arable,* or *wood-lands,* provided you work deep enough. " Be provided then (saith he) of three or four narrow " Spades about eight inches wide, and fifteen inches long, " with a Handle put into a Socket and Ring, with a " Tread round it, to set the foot upon to dig; and at " every twenty foot asunder, if the ground lie near a level, " dig a narrow trench of about ten inches, or a foot " wide at most, quite through, at twenty foot asunder, " and a full foot and half within the Clay: Then take " a wooden Rowl of about five inches diameter at one

" end

" end of four foot long, and four inches diameter at the
" other, and placing this rowl at the bottom of the trench,
" take the Clay you had before dug out, and with a
" Rammer ram it in round the rowl, which will form a
" perfect Tube : And the rowler being bigger at one end
" than the other, you may, by the help of a Chain
" fasten'd to the bigger end, pull it out of the Tube ; so
" that proceeding four foot at a time, you go through
" your Trenches from end to end, taking care to keep the
" Extremities of the Tube open. He saith, there should be
" a Handle of about four foot long mortis'd into the great
" end of the rowl, by which the Workmen shoggle about
" the rowl, so as to loosen it in the tube, by which means
" the rowl will be the easier drawn out by the Chain.
" But before that is done, you are to punch a Hole about
" three inches diameter through the ramm'd Clay upon the
" top of your rowl, through which perforation all the wa-
" ter is to pass that comes from the ground above, down
" into the underground Drain or Tube below : But still,
" to keep this perforated Hole open, small artificial fag-
" gots of green wood should be laid upon it, with a broad
" Tile at top, to secure it from any Impression that may
" come from above : And thus (saith he) you have a
" clayey Field as hollow and unfit to retain stagnated wa-
" ter as a Sieve. These Tubes he has known perform
" their office twelve years, even in plough'd Lands, where
" the disorder of horses might be suppos'd to spoil the
" whole Scheme. It costs about Twenty shillings an Acre,
" each Drain at about Twenty foot distance. ⌊ See *Swit-*
zer's Fruit-Garden.⌋

Arti-

Article VII.

A Steward on his Survey fhould narrowly watch and obferve, that the Tenants do not gather the *Cow-dung* together on heaps, in order firft to *dry* it, and then to *burn* it ; as is too frequently practis'd, both in *York-fhire* and *Lincoln-fhire,* where Fuel is fomething fcarce, to the no fmall damage and prejudice to the Farm. The ufing *Hogs-dung,* inftead of *Soap,* to wafh their Linnen, deferves fome notice, and fhould not be indulg'd to excefs.

Article VIII.

A Steward fhould likewife on his Surveys diligently obferve, whether any of the Tenants do pare and burn the Soil of any part of their Farms : For tho' this is a practice of late years brought up, and encourag'd by the Farmers, for their own immediate advantage, and by *Art* made to look *plaufible,* efpecially where Avarice or Indigence are addrefs'd to by prefent rewards ; yet, led by *long* Experience, and *certain* Knowledge, I am *fure* no-

I   thing

thing hath more tended to the *falling* of rents and the *ruine* of Eſtates than * *Denſhiring*, as it is call'd from its firſt practice in *Devonſhire* ; where they now own, by way of Proverb, that tho' it is good for the *Father*, it is bad for the *Son*. And what brings on the deſtruction of a Farm the ſooner, is the ſtill *viler* Practice of the Farmer, who too often ſows *Rape* after burning ; than which, there cannot be a greater Beggarer, eſpecially of good Land ; for it ſtrikes a deep root into the Soil, and quickly fetches out all (or moſt) of the terreſtrial matter fit for Vegetation ; inſomuch, that the Land ſo abus'd *ſeldom* or *never* is known to come to it ſelf again. And again ; While the Steward is watching to prevent Abuſes, he ſhould not neglect to reſtrain the Tenants from ſowing *Hemp*, *Flax*, *Woad*, *Weldt*, *Madder* ; and from planting *Hops* or *Potatoes* ; (except in ſmall quantities for their own private uſe.) ALL which Vegetables are very deſtructive to Land, becauſe *they breed no manure* ; they *take from*, but *give nothing back to* the Earth : For which reaſon the practice ſhould be diſcourag'd, and indeed not ſuffer'd, even on the beſt Land, without a very *valuable* † *Conſideration* made to the

---

* I have often met with rebukes from ſeveral Farmers, and others, who are fond of *Denſhiring*, or Burning of *good* as well as *bad* Land: And they have wonder'd that I ſhould be againſt this *Noble* Improvement (as they call it) ſince there is ſuch *vaſt* quantities of Poor Land in *England*, that have by a long continuance in Paſture contracted ſuch a ſowre Juice, that the Land would be worth *nothing* without *paring* and burning the Soil : And they have told me, they have (by this method) receiv'd ſuch Crops as would purchaſe the Inheritance of the Land. Suppoſing this to be true, yet I would have them conſider, that *all* or moſt of the *Nitrous Particles*, by this method, muſt be *drawn* from the Land, eſpecially when the practice is continued which is generally done ; and ſo conſequently they can never expect to receive *little* or no advantage from the Land for the future. Therefore the *ſureſt* way to improve ſuch Poor Land, is to turn it up with the Plough, and to ſow ſuch Seeds upon it as the nature of the Land requires, and to plough in the Crop at *Midſummer*. *NB.* This method is more fully treated of in the Appendix.

† See Stewards Accompt.

Landlord, not exceeding the term of Three Years at most. And, after that, the utmost care must be taken that the Land be laid down not in too high Ridges, and with a sufficient quantity of such Dung or Lime as can be got for breeding Grass and * swarding the Land: *Coal-ashes* and *Horse-dung* for heavy Land, and *Cow-dung, Lime,* or *Marle* for light Land.

Article IX.

IT is also the great Care and Duty of a Steward to see that whatsoever Manure, or materials for Manure, his Lord's Estate produces, such as † *Lime-stone, Marle, Coal-ashes, Kilp-ashes, Were, Shells,* or *Sea-sand,* &c. be only used and dispos'd of to his Lord's Tenants, and not to the Freeholders, or their Tenants round about; that these Privileges may appear to be real and valuable Advantages attending their Farms.

---

* As the 'foremention'd Lands is design'd to be continued for Pasture, so it is adviseable to sow them with the natural *Hay-seed,* allowing Ten or Fifteen Bushels to an Acre where it can conveniently be got, near any considerable City or Market-Town. This hath been practis'd with great success, because these natural Grasses do not wear out, as the artificial ones do.

† The disposing of the 'foremention'd Manure to the Freeholders round the Country, is practis'd *very* much by such Stewards who make *haste* to be *rich* by this Article, as well as many others mention'd in this Treatise.

Arti-

Article X.

A Steward fhould have a watchful Eye, that the Mole-catcher perform his duty in deftroying that noxi-ous Animal, efpecially in the Spring and breeding-time. Lazy Tenants are apt to think Moles do little or no Harm, and fo they are too often neglected : But fure I am, the mifchief is great where they are numerous ; for, in a dry Summer following, little Grafs will grow where the foil is much burrow'd and made hollow. Twelve-pence a dozen for what the Mole-catcher deftroys, is a better Bargain than to give yearly wages, becaufe it is a common practice for fuch Perfons to abufe the truft re-pofed in them, when they are paid by the year. It is alfo the care of the Steward to fee that each Tenant do level the Meadow and Pafture ground, as near as poffible in the *Spring*, and to fpread the Mole-heaps and Ant-banks, to prevent the ftroke of the Sythe's being inter-rupted, and hinder'd from coming too near the Ground ; it being an *undeniable Truth*, that one inch at the bottom is worth four at top.

Article XI.

A Steward should take care that no part of his Lord's Estate be stock'd with Rabbits, except it be on very large *Commons* or *Moors*, at least Three miles distant from Enclosures or Common-Fields. At Two miles distance they will often *strole* for food, to the great prejudice of the neighbouring Farmers, as well as to the Woods usually kept in hand. The mischief that has been done by Rabbits is very visible and remarkable, on his Grace the Duke of *Buckingham*'s Estate in *Lincoln-shire*; where the indolent Steward suffer'd the Tenants to stock their Farms with Rabbits upon a light blowing Sand, which when burrow'd by them, becomes easily subject to the violence of the Winds; and accordingly above One hundred and fifty Acres of good Land, of a neighbouring Farm, have been cover'd with a deep Sand in less than a year: But, since that, proper methods and due care have been taken to prevent the like damage, by keeping the Rabbits on the outside of the Estate; which may easily be continued with care and watchfulness; being well satisfied they may be kept within bounds by the common methods of *Ferreting* and *Netting*.

K   *Arti-*

Article XII.

A Steward fhould likewife be careful and vigilant that none of the Tenants do *let* any part of their Farms to *Under-Tenants* ; which I have known frequently pra-ctis'd with much *hurt* and *prejudice* to the Land. For tho' the chief Tenants themfelves are apt to cry out before they are hurt, yet I have made it my frequent Obfervation (as I have been upon my Surveys) that the Farmers are not a little *cruel* to one another, in *racking* up the Lands to twice the value; at which *exceffive* price they commonly *fet* it to an *Under-Tenant* ; which Extor-tion naturally puts the faid Under-Tenant upon ufing in-direct means to get the *heart* out of the Land : And yet that Lofs, in the end, of confequence falls hard on the Land-lord. But all pretences for doing this may in great mea-fure be prevented by the Steward's *Care*, in laying the Farms as *compact* together as poffible, that the Tenant may not be tempted to let any ufelefs part of his Farm to an Under-Tenant. Neither indeed fhould a Steward fuffer any of his Lord's Lands to be let to the *Freehold Tenants* within or near his Lord's Manor, becaufe 'tis a natural Contrivance, or piece of *Cunning*, in them to lay all or moft of their Manure upon their own Land, to the great *Improve-ment* of the one, and *Beggary* of the other : And, by vertue of this abominable CLOWN-CRAFT practice, when they think proper, and when their own turn is ferv'd, they'll give it up, as having already got what they intended.

Arti-

Article XIII.

A Steward, as much as in him lieth, and without Op-
pression, should endeavour to lay all the small Farms,
let to poor indigent People, to the great ones. But this
must be done with discretion, as it may be with Reason
and Justice, as the Heads of Families happen to fall, without continuing the Farms to the poor Remains, who may
as well betake themselves to other Employments; or if
unable, had better be provided for otherwise : And this
will be a means of keeping a multitude of Poor out of the
Parish, who generally care not to come where they must
live by hard Labour.

NEVERTHELESS, in some instances, and near any
populous trading Town, it may be very proper to let
Lands in small parcels to an inferiour *working* People, who
can make great Advantages by selling Milk ; or to a *trading* People, who will give more than it could be let for
otherwise, for their convenience ; chusing rather to have
provisions of their own at the best hand, than to go to
Market to buy at a dearer rate. I have known very considerable Improvements made on Noblemens Estates situa-
ted near the Sea, by granting Leases of the Ground for
building Houses upon the Waste, at an easie rate for the
first term of Ten or Twelve years, by way of encouragement ; and afterwards they have readily submitted

to

to a confiderable advance of rent for a fecond term ; by which means the Place by degrees foon became very populous, ready for a Charter to be made a trading Market-Town, and at the fame time able to fix advanc'd Rents (even double to their former value) on all the neighbouring Eftates. This noble Example of good Husbandry having been compleated by that great Oeconomift Sir *Walter Caverly,* near *Leeds* in *York-fhire,* (whofe beautiful Seat ftands upon the River *Air*) fhould animate and encourage Others to the like Improvements, who, by laying out confiderable Sums of Money in building *Fulling-Mills* upon the River, has tempted the Cloth-makers to come and fettle there with their Families; infomuch that his Eftate and Lands round about quickly advanc'd, and doubled the old rent.

Article XIV.

A Steward fhould not forget to make the beft Enquiry into the difpofition of any of the Freeholders within or near any of his Lord's Manors, to fell their Lands, that he may ufe his beft Endeavours to purchafe them at as reafonable a price as may be for his Lord's Advantage and Convenience. Some Inftances there have been of Stewards, who, after they have made *hafte* to be rich, have made thefe Enquiries for *their own* fakes, and have purchas'd out the Freeholders, thereby making an Eftate for themfelves, even within their own Lord's Manors;
info-

infomuch that fometimes I have known it fo order'd that
the Lord's Tenants have been call'd to do Suit and Service at his own Court : But, for the fake of *Honour* and
Honefty, I hope thefe Inftances are rare; and fo I content my felf to have given this hint, ftill perfwading the
vigilant Steward to be zealous, for his Lord's fake, in
purchafing all the Freeholders out as foon as poffible, efpecially in fuch Manors where Improvements are to be made
by *inclofing* Commons and Common-Fields; which (as
every one, who is acquainted with the late Improvements
in Agriculture, muft know) is not a little advantageous
to the Nation in general, as well as highly profitable to
the Undertaker. If the Freeholders cannot *all* be perfwaded to fell, yet at leaft an Agreement for *Inclofing* fhould
be pufh'd forward by the Steward, and a Scheme laid,
wherein it may appear, that an exact and proportional
fhare will be allotted to every Proprietor; perfwading
them firft, if poffible, to fign a Form of Agreement, and
then to chufe Commiffioners on both fides.

IF the Steward be a Man of good fenfe, he will find
a neceffity for making ufe of it all, in rooting out *Super-
ftition* from amongft them, as what is fo great a hindrance to all *noble* Improvements. The fubftance of what
is proper for the Proprietors to fign before an Inclofure is
to be made, may be conceiv'd in fome fuch Form as followeth.

 "WHEREAS it is found, by long Experience, that
" Common or open Fields, where-ever they are fuffer'd
" or continued, are great Hindrances to a publick Good,
" and the honeft Improvement which every one might
" make of his own, by diligence and a feafonable charge:

L   " And

" And whereas the common Objections hitherto rais'd
" againſt Incloſures are founded on miſtakes, as if Incloſures
" contributed either to hurt or ruine the Poor; whilſt it is
" plain that (when an Incloſure is once reſolv'd on) the
" Poor will be imploy'd for many years in planting and
" preſerving the Hedges, and afterwards will be ſet to
" work both in the Tillage and Paſture, wherein they
" may get an honeſt livelihood.   And whereas all or moſt
" the Inconveniencies and Misfortunes which uſually at-
" tend the *open Waſtes* and common Fields have been fatal-
" ly experienc'd at ————, to the great diſcouragement
" of Induſtry and good Husbandry in the Freeholders, *viz.*
" That the Poor take their Advantage to pilfer and ſteal and
" treſpaſs; That the Corn is ſubject to be ſpoil'd by Cat-
" tle, that ſtray out of the Commons and Highways adja-
" cent; That the Tenants or Owners, if they would ſe-
" cure the fruits of their labours to themſelves, are obli-
" ged either to keep exact time in ſowing and reaping, or
" elſe to be ſubject to the damage and inconvenience that
" muſt attend the *lazy* practices of thoſe who ſow unſea-
" ſonably, ſuffering their Corn to ſtand to the beginning
" of Winter, thereby hind'ring the whole Pariſh from eat-
" ing the Herbage of the common Field till the Froſts
" have ſpoil'd the moſt of it.   For theſe Reaſons, and
" for many more which might be aſſign'd to encourage
" Induſtry, and to aſcertain a ſecurity to every Man of
" enjoying the quiet poſſeſſion of his Labour and Care,
" we whoſe Names are underwritten, being Freeholders,
" do agree to the Incloſing, and to the immediate ſetting
" about the work of an Incloſure in the common Fields
" of ————, and to bring it to perfection with all conve-
" nient ſpeed.

NB. I

NB. I have often lamented the Misfortune that attends Noblemen's and Gentlemen's Eſtates, where only a *part* of the Common Fields have been incloſ'd, becauſe the Tenants carry *all* or moſt of the Manure bred upon the incloſ'd part, to the *Fallows* in the Common Fields ; which indeed *want* it, becauſe they are conſtantly kept in Tillage : Yet, nevertheleſs, this unequal management impoveriſhes the incloſ'd part *not a little* ; therefore the moſt effectual way to prevent this *growing Evil,* is to endeavour (as ſoon as poſſible) to incloſe the *whole* : Till this is perform'd, the Steward ſhould ſee that the Tenants ſpend the quantity of Manure bred on the incloſ'd part upon the Land which produced it, in order to reſtore (in ſome meaſure) the *Riches* that *conſtant* mowing may have taken from the Meadows.

Article XV.

IT is another conſiderable part of the duty of a Steward, whenever an Offer is made of ſelling an Eſtate adjoyning upon his Lord's other Manors, to go to every one of the Tenants, endeavouring to ſee all their Acquittances for as *many* years paſt as poſſible, that he may be able to acquaint his Lord if it is an old-rented Eſtate ; and if any Advance hath been made, he will by that means ſee what it is. It hath been a practice of late years, not

much

much to be commended, to R A C K up the Tenants beyond what the Eftate will bear, in order to fell it with
advantage; which method is not ftrictly *honeft*. And I
have likewife found it too frequently practis'd, before an
Eftate is to be fold, provided the Tenants will but agree
to give an advanc'd rent, the Landlord privately confents
to pay what the Tenant paid before, *viz.* the *Poor's*, the
Church, and the *Conftable's* Affeffments ; and it is not feldom that, befides thefe, a fum of money is given into
the bargain : Whereas, if a Steward is *vigilant* and careful, thefe private Contracts tending to over-rate the value of the Eftate, may in great meafure be difcover'd ;
and that difcovery will be of fuch real fervice to his
Lord, that it will prevent his being impos'd upon in a
Purchafe.

Article XVI.

A Steward fhould ever have a watchful Eye upon all
the feveral Farm-Houfes belonging to his Lord
within the Manor, and under his Care, to fee they are
kept up in good repair. When an Improvement is made
upon an Eftate, and new Leafes granted, it is cuftomary
that the Lord of the Manor be at the expence of putting the
Houfes, *&c.* in tenantable repair ; but, after that, 'tis highly
reafonable that they fhould be kept fo by the Tenants, efpecially

cially being allow'd rough Timber to do the same, which yet should be assign'd them by the Steward himself, and no leave given to the Tenant to haggle and cut where and what he pleases; as hath been too frequently practis'd under a pretended and mistaken notion, that they ought to have an Allowance for *Plough-boot*, *Cart-boot*, and *Fire-boot*, &c. a Custom formerly indeed allow'd to such Tenants who had Leases for Three Lives, and likewise to Copyhold Tenants upon Lives, but very seldom to Tenants at *Will*, and short Leases for a term of Years. These rules being duely observ'd by a Steward, will not only be a means to preserve the Woods, but also prevent any Bills for repairs of Houses for the future, which commonly prove no inconsiderable Burthen, and has been indeed a sort of *Tax* upon Noblemen's Estates.

THE like Reasoning should take place, and be allow'd with respect to Water-Mills and Wind-Mills, which, generally speaking, are the *worst* part of an Estate; especially as the matter is now order'd, when Custom prevails to oblige the Landlord to find Mill-stones, Wheels, and Coggs, with all other Utensils proper and belonging to Mills, which continually wearing out, are constantly one or other of them wanted. To prevent therefore this constant Demand and annual Rent-charge, as well as the Repairs of the Mill and Out-Houses, I have all along (where I have been concern'd in the Valuing and IMPROVING Estates) agreed for the *best* and *most* improv'd Rent I could get; at the same time obliging the Miller by Covenant to be at ALL the abovemention'd charges, having first put the Mills and Appurtenances in sufficient repair; after which I suffer'd them to take a long Lease of Twenty-one years. And, to make matters still easier, in some parts of the North, where

M the

the *Land-Tax* is not exceffive, I have agreed with ALL the Tenants for a clear Rent, themfelves paying ALL Taxes and Affeffments whatfoever. Such Advice and Practice I founded upon this reafoning; That thefe and the abovemention'd Difburfements being left out of Accompts, would prove of great Eafe to Noblemen and Gentlemen in the examining them, as well as of great Satisfaction to their Minds, when they fee in one view what their real Eftates are, and what they can command upon all Emergencies, without unknown and endlefs Deductions. Every Steward therefore fhould be perfwaded to govern himfelf by thefe Rules, as of great Ufe and Eafe to himfelf in making up his Accompts, exclufive of this Confideration, that it will recommend his Diligence alfo, by making it appear, that he ftudies both his Lord's Eafe and his *Intereft*.

Article XVII.

WHEN a Tenant's Term or Leafe is out, or that he happens to leave his Farm, 'tis the Steward's Bufinefs to fee that he doth not *overftock* his Pafture and Meadows before the time of expiration, whether it be *Lady-day* or *May-day*, by taking in more Cattle than his own by way of JOYSTING; which is a practice contrary to both *Law* and *Juftice*. In moft parts of the North of *England*, and in many others, *May-day* is the

time

time of *Entering* and *Leaving*, which makes the Steward's Care to prevent Abuses the more neceſſary, becauſe *over-ſtocking* the Meadows at a time when they ſhould be *growing* and getting head to defend themſelves from the Drought and ſcorching Summer's Sun, is a great Injury to a new Tenant. I have known Meadows ſo manag'd and left, tho' worth Thirty ſhillings an Acre, have been ſo bare and ſcorch'd, that they have not produced above half a Load of Hay from an Acre : A Loſs that bears no compariſon to the unjuſt Gain of the preceeding greedy Tenant. It were indeed, on all accounts, much to be wiſh'd that the Cuſtom and Practice of eating the Meadows till *May-day*, ſo hurtful and inconvenient in it ſelf, and ſo ſubject to be abus'd, were broken and alter'd for the better and more reaſonable term of *Lady-day* ; but till that can be effected with prudence, and without clamour, the ſtronger will be the Argument for the Steward's greater vigilance and care to prevent Abuſes.

UNDER this Article it may be proper to obſerve, that great Care ſhould be taken that the Tenants ſell off their Farms as little Hay and Straw as poſſible ; on the contrary, that they be oblig'd to ſpend the ſame on the Premiſes : But yet if it ſhould ſo happen, that in a ſcarce time a great demand for Hay is made ; or, that the Tenant lives near *London*, or any other conſiderable Market-Town, where the price of Hay and Straw will make a good advance in his rent, the Sale may be permitted ; provided at the ſame time the moſt diligent care be taken, by *ſtrict* Articles and Covenants, that he ſupply the Loſs and Damage by purchaſing at leaſt Three Loads of rotten Dung mix'd with Earth, for every One Load of Hay carried off the Premiſes, over and above what was made there. But ſtill,

ſtill, notwithſtanding ſome of theſe Exceptions, the general Rule ſhould in the main take place, and be obſerv'd, (eſpecially where there's no Dung to be got but what the Premiſes afford) *viz.* To ſell no Hay or Straw, but to ſpend the ſame upon the Premiſes. And becauſe 'tis plain and certain, from Experience, that conſtant mowing of Meadows is not only apt to weaken the Soil, but to produce ſowre and coarſe Graſs ; the Steward ſhould oblige the Tenant to alter the property, turning ſometimes Paſture into Meadow, and Meadow into Paſture ; but yet by no means to ſuffer the Tenant to *encreaſe* the Meadow and *leſſen* the Paſture, eſpecially at his leaving the Farm.

NEITHER at ſuch a time ſhould it be forgot, that the Tenant be oblig'd to leave a ſufficient quantity of Tillage (*viz.* about a third part) to the ſucceeding Tenant, well fallow'd in a ſeaſonable and Husband-like manner by four Tilts or Ploughings, the ſucceeding Tenant being by * Cuſtom generally willing to allow about Eight or Nine ſhillings an Acre, where 'tis the Cuſtom to enter at *Michaelmas,* for ſuch Fallows ; ſtill ever bearing in mind, that the departing Tenant be oblig'd alſo to leave all the Straw and Dung bred and made the preceding year to the new Tenant, without any conſideration or reward for the ſame, as agreeable to Reaſon, and ought to be a General Cuſtom.

---

* In ſome parts of the North, where 'tis the cuſtom for new Tenants to enter at *Lady day,* the departing Tenant requires his *way-going Crop* of Corn ; which is a hardſhip on the new Tenant ; but in other parts it is *more reaſonable,* the departing Tenant requires but two thirds of the Crop for his charge of Fallowing, Sowing, &c. The former cuſtom ſhou'd (by the Steward) be aboliſh'd, and the latter *encourag'd.*

Arti-

Article XVIII.

BEcaufe it is a moft fatal and too general an *Evil* to fuffer Mounds and Hedges to decay, either thro' negligence or want of Skill, to the great hurt and finking of Eftates, a Steward, in his Surveys, fhould have a conftant Eye upon the Tenant's method of cutting and plafhing the Hedges, directing them not to chop and haggle them in an unskilful unfightly manner, as the too common practice (of the North efpecially) is, but to lay the branches * *horizontally*; which will quickly tend to thicken the Hedge, and fill up all Vacancies and Gaps : And alfo to cut out all the larger Wood that can be fpar'd, leaving the part fmooth and floping, twifting fome Bryars on the top, to keep every thing in its place. A difcreet and skilful management of Hedges is a confiderable Article of a Steward's Care, becaufe it tends not only to prevent Gaps, and uneafie trefpaffes of one Tenant upon another, but alfo to the longer continuance and duration of the Stools and Thorns of the Hedge it felf. In cutting off all projecting branches, which tend to fowre the Grafs, the Workman fhould regard that the ftroke of the Hatchet go UPWARDS and not DOWNWARDS; and that fuch other Branches as lie convenient for thickening the Hedge, and muft be bent

---

* See Fig. 2d.

N   down-

downwards, be not cut more than half through ; wherein carelefs Workmen are apt to tranfgrefs, to the great damage of the Hedge.

WORKMEN alfo, in the management of Hedges, and plafhing them, fhould be advertis'd to drive down * Stakes. at about five or fix foot diftance in all thin parts of the Hedge, which will much tend both to ftrengthen and thicken it, till the *horizontal* Branches get ftrength and fulnefs to do that office themfelves. There fhould be more than ordinary Care taken in the management of *old* Hedges; not to cut the Heads entirely off, and leave the Stools like fo many *Pollards*, as the hafty way in the North is, but rather to cut out as much of the *old* Wood as is poffible and to preferve ALL the beft of the *young*.

THIS is a proper place to advertife the Steward, that he be always prepar'd and furnifh'd with a Nurfery of Quicks, that he may not be oblig'd to go to Market when a demand is made for Quantities upon new Inclofures, or dividing others within his Lord's Manors. His way is, to provide in Autumn five or fix Bufhels of *Haws*, letting

---

* It may not be amifs to relate here the Method which a notable Farmer took to prevent his Hedge-ftakes from being ftolen ; [and, in a fcarce Country for Fuel, this is a Grievance which requires their utmoft Care and Invention to prevent.] His Way was ; By the help of a large Nail-piercer, he bored holes flantwife in feveral of the faireft and moft tempting Stakes, then filling the holes with Gunpowder, and pegging them up very faft; and, to prevent any fufpicion of a Defign, he dawb'd the part over with Dirt, and then left them ftanding in a carelefs manner. The Defign quickly took, and the Stakes were gone ; fo it may be guefs'd it was not long before the Rumour of a *Porridge-pot* being like to be blown up was got about the Parifh. And this Effect was certain that ever after his Hedges were preferv'd from Robbers.

them

them lie on a heap in fome by-place out of doors till the Autumn following, (for they will not grow till the fecond year) and then, in a Nurfery of mellow ground, about a quarter of an Acre, (more or lefs as there is a demand for 'em) they may be fow'd, after the Land is dug up with the Spade, in fmall ridges, for the better con-veniency of *weeding* ; and in two or three years time, accor-ding to the goodnefs of the Soil, they will be fit for tranf-planting and ufe.

THIS frugal provident Method fhould be encourag'd, not only as it faves his Lord's Money, but as it anfwers better than the common way of getting *ftunted* mifhapen plants out of the Woods. And it is to be remember'd alfo, that the Steward, having a full ftock and quantity of his own at home, will not fuffer him to think much to al-low a fufficient Number for all purpofes. A miftaken frugality has been of ill confequence in the North, where they plant only *one row* of Quicks, becaufe where a failure happens, there is fure to be a Gap ; whereas, where there are *two rows*, (as there ever fhould be) if either of them hit, that misfortune is prevented, and the deficiency is fup-ply'd either from the *upper* or the *under* row.

WHEN the provident Steward has furnifh'd himfelf with a Nurfery of Quicks, as above, he fhould endeavour and contrive to *inclofe*, and thereby *leffen*, all fuch large Paftures and Meadows as contain thirty or forty Acres, or more ; for, by leffening and dividing fuch, they will be much im-prov'd every way, efpecially as they are made capable the better to *winter* their Cattle, and to defend them from the extremities of the cold Winds, Storms, and driving Snows : For want of fuch convenient fhelters, I have known large

tracts

tracts of Land, only bounded by diſtant and extended Hedges by the *Trent* ſide, to ſuffer very much, becauſe the Tenants were forced to winter them at home, which of conſequence oblig'd them to carry the Hay along with 'em, the produce whereof was commonly forgot to be brought back in Manure, but rather too often carried and laid upon the *Tillage* nearer home, to the great damage and impoveriſhment of the Meadows and Paſtures.

In *Devonſhire* they are very extraordinary Husbands in this way, as well as many others, wherein they ſhould be imitated; for it is rare and remarkable there to find a Paſture or Meadow Ground above eight or ten Acres: But then they are alſo very exemplary and diligent in their exact laying and plaſhing their Hedges, in order to make them thick and impenetrable, not ſuffering the large branches to project and hang over, which would ſpoil and ſowre a good part of the ground where the Incloſures are ſmall.

To conclude this Head, I would adviſe the Steward, when an Incloſure is to be made, not to be too *raſh* in † planting Timber-trees, of any ſort, eſpecially *Aſhes*, in the Hedge-rows; for all of them tend to impoveriſh the Land by their ſpreading roots, and by their projecting branches (the wet dropping from them) do much hurt to the Hedges, as well as to the Soil, by ſowring the Graſs.

---

† I hope the latter part of this Article will not be ſo underſtood as if I was for diſcouraging the *noble* Improvements of planting Timber-trees.

The hint I have given in this Article is only to ſhew the neceſſity of planting Timber-trees by themſelves, becauſe it is now pretty well known, that the ſpreading branches do no ſmall damage to large Underwoods, as well as Hedge-rows.

Arti-

An Hedge of about

The same Hedge Cut b

The same Hedge th

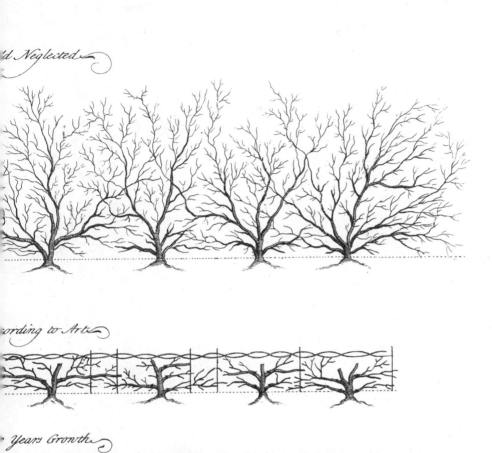

…ld *Neglected*

…ording to *Art*

…Years *Growth*

Article XIX.

A Steward, on his Survey, fhould not be unmindful to enquire, and by proper marks and tokens to obferve, whether there be any *Coal, Tin,* or *Lead*-Mines within his Lord's Manors, thefe being oft-times greater Riches *under* ground than the beft Improvements *above.* Wherefore a timely and faithful account of all (even the Probabilities of) thefe Treafures fhould be related, that Tryals may be made, firft by *boring,* and then by *finking* Pits. However, it may be neceffary to add, that the Borer be narrowly watch'd, to prevent the *Coal-owners* from all parts, and others, whofe intereft it is to *ftifle* thefe Enquiries, from tampering with him, and ufing fuch indirect and unlawful Arts as tend to make *abortive* all fuch honeft Endeavours both for a publick and private Good. The fame diligence in the Steward fhould be extended to the difcovery of all *Quarries* that happen to lie within his Lord's Manors; for if they prove to be of a good and fine fort of Free-ftone, and efpecially if near the Sea-coaft or a navigable River, fuch Quarry frequently tends to no inconfiderable Advancement of his Lord's Eftate.

O   *Article*

Article XX.

IT is not only neceſſary that a Steward ſhould be a good Accomptant, but alſo that he ſhould have a tolerable degree of Skill in *Mathematicks*, Surveying, Mechanicks, and Architecture ; for in every one of thoſe Particulars his Ingenuity and Skill will be upon many occaſions call'd upon and made uſe of. And he ſhould likewiſe endeavour to make himſelf maſter of the true ∗ Prices of all ſorts of Work relating to Husbandry, that he be not impos'd upon, or oblig'd to watch the Day-workmen, which commonly proves the moſt chargeable method. A Steward then thus qualified, before he engageth in any Work of conſequence, relating either to *Incloſures*, or *Architecture*, or *Draining*, &c. ſhould firſt ſend as exact an Eſtimate as poſſible, what the ſame will amount to, that his Lord may *ſit down and count the Coſt*, and make a deliberate Judgment, whether the Charge will anſwer his Expectations in the propos'd Benefit. And becauſe upon every Eſtate lying at ſome diſtance one from another, it is on many accounts very neceſſary that a Villa or Country-Houſe ſhould be built, the Steward ſhould uſe his beſt Skill (or by the aſſiſtance of

---

∗ See the latter end of Stewards Accompts.

the

the beſt * Architect) in drawing out the Particulars of the Charge of doing the ſame, aiming not ſo much at *State* as *Convenience*; *i. e.* juſt ſo as to anſwer his Uſe and Diverſion in the Summer.

I cannot but think every Contrivance right, and every Convenience fit to be encourag'd, which tend to *invite* the Lord of the Manor himſelf ſometimes to come down and *viſit* his Eſtate, that his *Intereſt* and his Diverſions may give a Reliſh to one another. His own Ingenuity and Contrivance added to his Steward's *Care*, will quickly introduce *Politeneſs* into his Country, and tend to ſet ſuch Examples of *Improvements* and good Husbandry, as will make him *belov'd* and popular, at the ſame time when he is furniſh'd with larger Abilities to ſupply his *own* and his Country's *Wants*.

---

* The Example of the noted Architect Mr. *Morris*, and ſome few others, ſhould be a pattern to the reſt, to be *punctual*, to make their *Calculations* ſo, as to undertake the building of a Nobleman's or Gentleman's Seat according to the Deſign firſt made and *calculated*; and not as too many have done, who have told Noblemen, &c. the Charge of building a Seat, according to their calculation, for *Twenty thouſand Pounds*; but before the Building was finiſh'd, they found, to their *Sorrow*, that it coſt them near Fifty thouſand Pounds. *NB.* I have known a very neat Country-houſe, juſt fit for a Nobleman, &c. when he comes down to look into his affairs, built for leſs than Three thouſand Pounds.

Arti-

Article XXI.

AFter a Steward hath diligently furvey'd his Lord's Eftate, and hath made himfelf mafter of the method which every Tenant takes to raife his Rent, and to provide for his Family, he fhould alfo carefully obferve the Crops and ftocks of Cattle that each Tenant hath upon the feveral forts of Land, whether Arable, Pafture, or Meadow; by which means (always fuppofing him to be well vers'd in Country affairs) he'll be able to judge, not only what Care hath been ufed to *improve* and advance, and what Neglects have been fuffer'd to diminifh the Products, but alfo how many Quarters of the feveral forts of Grain each Acre one with another on Tillage produces; and how many Loads of Hay come from the Meadows. He fhould likewife confider (and, if need be, *direct*) what ftock of Cattle of all forts each Tenant's Farm will maintain, that he may be a conftant cheque upon them, that they do keep a *fufficient* Stock; for a deficiency in that kind is as fatal and hurtful to the Farmer's Intereft as *over-ftocking*: Accordingly I have known many a Farmer fink and fail in the World meerly for want of a *fufficient* Stock, altho' they have had very *cheap* Bargains : And indeed a certain truth it is, confirm'd by Experience, that an *over-cheap* Bargain and Farm many times tends to indulge the Farmer in Luxury and Idlenefs, and to make him VIE

with

with Gentlemen, and thofe that have Eſtates of their own, in their way of living and the bringing up their Families : And when thefe Follies and abfurd ways of Living have reduced them to Poverty, the neceſſary confequence is, that the Farm (cheap as it is) is made *poor* too, and the Farmer cannot raife his Rents, becaufe there is a defect of Stock, both as to number and Goodnefs.

A careful provident Farmer, that keeps well his Accompts, and wifely balanceth his Gain and Lofs, if he would be affur'd that he gets by his Farm, and thrives in the World, muſt fell ✱ *two Rents* at the leaſt off the Premifes one year with another. Indeed the Farmers in *Kent, Eſſex,* and other Southern Counties round *London,* us'd to make it a Maxim, that *three* rents fhould be fold ; the confequence of which was, that if they rented Two or Three hundred Pounds a year, they quickly purchas'd Eſtates of their own, and let them to Tenants, who were forced to be content to fell *two rents* off the Premifes.

BEFORE a Steward makes his laſt Judgment of the value of a Farm, he fhould be well and exactly inform'd what the neighbouring Gentlemen or Freeholders let *their* Lands for by the Acre, and then the noble Rule of COMPARISON ufed difcreetly, will give a fanction to his Office and Duty, making allowances on both fides for better and worfe, either on *fome,* or on *many* accounts.

✱ 'Tis fuppos'd that the Tenant is to maintain his Family with fuch Provifions as his Farm produceth, and to fell two Rents off the Premifes, but not to fpend in an extravagant manner one Rent, or more, as too many have done, to their fudden failure, altho' they have a good pennyworth.

A due

A due regard had to this and the foregoing Rules would, I am perſwaded, be a good Foundation for forming a Judgment of the true Value of Eſtates, in order to their being let to the ſatisfaction of both Landlord and Tenant, which ſhould always be effected, if poſſible, that there may be no juſt Foundation for Complaint on either ſide: For altho' the Lord's Eſtate ought to be let to the beſt advantage, yet it ſhould be let without *racking* the induſtrious Tenant; as hath been too frequently done with *Art* and *Cunning* enough in ſome Stewards, in order to hide and conceal other unrighteous practices: But ſuch *racking*, on what pretence ſoever it be done, ever tends to the *diſſervice*, as well as to the *Diſcredit* of Perſons of Quality, ſeveral of whom, to my knowledge, have repented of being *led* into that miſtake, as having ſuſtain'd great Trouble and Loſs in their Rents. Some Inſtances I have known (eſpecially in the North, where the Farms are ſmall) of poor Tenants, who, rather than be turn'd off to ſeek their Living, will promiſe more than they are really able to perform.

I have been the longer on this Head with a view of making the *Truth* of theſe *Facts*, founded on Experience, take the deeper impreſſion on all Noblemen and Gentlemen, as of the laſt conſequence to their real Intereſt, and the Improvement of their Eſtates.

MOREOVER, as it hath appear'd to be a matter of great conſequence, that proper methods be uſed by the Steward, in order to let his Lord's Lands to the beſt advantage, ſo it is likewiſe proper to take notice here, that if the Steward doth not take care that the Tenants *keep up* the Farms in a due courſe of Husbandry, there will be no ſmall danger of the Rents ſinking again, even from an Advance

vance made and founded on modern Knowledge and rational Improvements. To prevent therefore this undesirable Circumstance, the Steward should see and insist upon it, that the Tenants do, every one of them, really and punctually perform the Covenants which they themselves have agreed to in their Leases. This is a matter of no *inconsiderable* consequence; for I have known Instances of Gentlemen's Estates sinking very much by irregular and *uncovenanted* practices, whilst the Tenants (by *neglect* or oversight) have been suffer'd to plow up fresh Pasture and Meadow, to *pare* and *burn* and *worry* out the strength of the Land by sowing *Rape*, &c. the consequence whereof hath been, that when they have throughly *impoverish'd* the Farm, and thus *eat* out the Life and *Heart* of it, they have thrown it back into the Lord's hand, where it commonly *sticks*.

IN the * Covenants of their Leases there should therefore be a *penalty* laid to each Covenant, to be paid *over* and above their *yearly rent*, which being intended to prevent Abuses, is recoverable by *Law*; whereas the common way of inserting Covenants into Leases (except a Bond is given, and the Tenants find Security) proves of little or no use, for want of a power to *force* and compel the execution.

As for the Farms of Eight or Ten pounds *per annum*, I have always found it to be of little moment to lease

---

* I have always found, where-ever I have been concern'd in agreeing with Tenants and drawing up Covenants, that they have *more readily* agreed to sign such Leases where a Penalty was laid to each Covenant, to be paid over and above the yearly Rent for non-performance, than to sign such Leases, where they are oblig'd to give Bond, and also to find security.

such,

leafe fuch, becaufe the Tenants that rent them are generally poor and neceffitous : Wherefore the beft way to deal with them, when they do not perform, or tranfgrefs their duty, is, firft to *reprove* them for not obferving good Rules, and when there is little hopes of their doing better, to get *rid* of them as foon as poffible, always fuppofing that fome care be taken of their Families, in fetting them to work in fuch ways which they better underftand.

ALTHO' I have not yet laid before the Steward and his Lord every part of a Steward's duty, yet, by what hath been already faid, it fufficiently appears, that to perform thefe and all the following Articles as they ought to be perform'd, with Fidelity and conftant Care, will take up almoft his whole time, without much room for Diverfions. I could wifh all Noblemen and Gentlemen, for their own *Honour* and *Intereft*, would be perfwaded to make fomething larger allowances of Salary than are ufually given : I do not fay that large Wages makes a man *honeft* ; but I am fatisfied that a *too ftrict*, and therefore *miftaken* notion of *faving Oeconomy*, with refpect to a Steward's ftanding Wages, hath oft-times been the Occafion of *corrupting* the Steward, and putting him upon indirect means to get where and what he ought not ; which proves in the end the *deareft Bargain* to thofe who think themfelves *wife in their generation*.

IN fhort, there fhould no one Circumftance relating to the Office and Duty of a Steward be made a Gain to Him, but the whole fhould accrue, and ought to be accounted to his Lord, whofe wifdom it fhould be to make the *Salary* an ample Reward for his *faithful* Labours.

Arti-

Article XXII.

A Steward should make strict Enquiry after all *Poachers*, that destroy the Game within his Lord's Manors, and when they are found and known, to lay regular Complaints before the next Justice of the Peace, that they may be prosecuted and punish'd according to Law. And also if there be any found not qualified to keep Greyhounds, Guns, Setting-dogs, Nets, &c. he should be diligent in informing against them, that their Dogs and Guns, &c. may be taken away from 'em ; the pursuit of these sorts of Games being observ'd, in the lower sort of People, to be the effect of Idleness, the consequence whereof is neglect of their proper business, which ends in poverty, and oftentimes something worse. However, on all accounts, the Game ought to be preserv'd by the diligence and care of the Steward and Game-keeper, for the sake of their Lord's Diversion and his Table. Indeed every temptation should be encourag'd that tends to invite Noblemen and others to visit their Estates in Person every Summer ; for, without such presence, whatever others may think who have not a sense of it, I who know the Misfortunes and Losses that have happen'd by continued Absence, must *averr*, That nothing has tended more to the Abuse and Ruin of brave Estates, than the Lord's neglect of looking *himself* sometimes into his own affairs ; whereas, on the contrary, I have

Q   always

always found his presence to have been a constant cheque both upon Steward and Tenant, as to any *unjustifiable* Connivances or private Bargains. Where-ever therefore I have been concern'd, I have, with pretty good success, inculcated this Advice and Maxim (supported by the foregoing reasons) of *Occasional Residence*.

Article XXIII.

A GAIN: It is the duty, and should be the Care of a Steward, to make himself master of all the ancient * Customs belonging to his Lord's Manors; which Knowledge will enable him to keep them up, and to prevent their oblivion. As for instance; (1.) It is customary in most Manors for the Tenants to send their Teams to lead home the Hay and Corn which comes off the Demesne Lands commonly kept in hand for the use of the Lord of the Manor, when he comes in the Summer to live among his Tenants. (2.) It is also customary for the Tenants to send their Teams to lead Timber and Stone, &c. whenever there is occasion for building or Repairs. (3.) It is also a good-natur'd Custom for each Tenant to send every

---

* The Steward, at his first entering upon his Office, should get a Copy of the Customs from the Ancientest Court Rolls, in order to make himself master of the ancient Customs of the several Manors.

year,

year, during their Lord's Refidence, a Prefent of two fat Capons or Turkeys; or elfe any other prefent of Fifh or Fowl, fuch as the Country produceth, of the like value. (4.) It is common for each Tenant to keep a couple of Hounds or Setting-Dogs for the ufe of the Lord when he comes down, for his diverfion.

IT may not be amifs here to advertife the Steward to take care, where the Freehold-Tenants have a Townfhip entire to themfelves, that they do not encroach upon the Lord's Wafte, by digging *Stone*, *Sand*, &c. expofing the fame to fale, when it is none of their right : And when there is any want of fubmiffion and acknowledgment of the Offence, to make Examples of one or two by a Profecution, to deter others from offending in the like manner.

I have known Inftances, where the Freeholders have in-clos'd the Lord's Wafte down to the Sea-fide, infomuch that in procefs of time they have gain'd confiderable quantities of Land, and were beginning to difpute even the Privi-leges of the Lord ; nay, and have fometimes claim'd a right to all the Advantages along the Sea-coaft, fo far as their encroach'd Inclofure reach'd, fuch as *Wrecks* and *Strays*. Herein appears alfo the neceffity of an *occafional Refi-dence*.

THE like care fhould be taken by every Steward with relation to fuch Eftates as are let out upon Lives, whe-ther Leafehold or Copyhold, (a Cuftom much ufed in the Weft of *England*) that a ftrict Enquiry be made at the Death of a Tenant, whether the beft Goods, or the beft Beaft, which is due to the Lord of the Manor by way of *Harriot*, is not clandeftinely convey'd away by thofe who

who think it no Sin to cheat either the *Lord* or the *Parson*, but applaud themselves for being *witty* in giving it a new Name, and *cunning* in keeping secret what will not bear the Light. The Steward therefore should be as watchful and circumspect as may be, to prevent Frauds: Not but that, at the same time, if an honest and fair discovery of the truth could be obtain'd, I would advise every Lord of *such* Manors as consist of Copyholders of Inheritance, not to be too † rigid and exact on the account of *Harriots*, because the severity of it discourageth the Tenants in buying and selling those Estates to one another, and so consequently lessens a considerable Income by *Fines* and *Surrenders*, which is no small part of the Lord's casual Profits arising from the several Manors, especially where the Tenants are numerous, as it most commonly happens when Lands are held by the 'foremention'd Tenure.

To conclude this Article about Customs, I would advise all Noblemen and Gentlemen, whose Tenants hold their Lands by *Copy of Court-Roll* for three Lives, not to let them renew, except they will agree to deliver up their Copy, in order to alter the Tenure, by converting it to *Leasehold on Lives*. This method will put a stop to that *unreasonable Custom* of the W I D O W's holding a Life by her *Free-bench*, which is a *fourth* Life, not covenanted for in the Copy, but only pretended to by *Custom*; which deprives the Lord of an undoubted right of making the best, and *doing what he will with his own*.

---

† I remember an Instance of a Lord of a Manor that would always take the Harriots in kind, such as Jewels, Plate, &c. but he found his mistake, in a few years, by the lessening of the casual Profits by Surrenders, &c.

Arti-

Article XXIV.

WHERE the Lord of the Manor is the *Impropriator* of the Livings of the several Parishes, and consequently has the great *Tythes* to dispose of as he seeth fit, it is the Steward's Wisdom and Care to let the several great Tythes, either in *whole* or in *parcels*, to such Tenants as have the *worst* Land, or are furthest remote from the conveniency of *dung* and proper Manure, never suffering them, on any consideration, to be let to the *Freeholders*, tho' Tenants; because they will be sure to enrich their own Lands therewith, and let their Farms shift for themselves, especially when their Leases are near expiring, that then they intend to get the heart out of the Land, and afterwards give it up into the hand of the Lord to make the best of it. If the Parishes or Townships from whence Tythes are due are of any extent, it is hardly to be imagin'd what Riches they will afford to the Impropriator's Farms, discreetly parcel'd out, by means of the Hay, Straw, &c. brought home from every quarter, and loaded out again in Dung, over and above the usual quantity made on a Farm. And to prevent any future loss or decay in this advantageous Article of *Tythes,* the Steward should ever be upon his watch, to prevent (if possible) the Freeholders inclosing any part of their Land in the common Fields, which commonly ends in lessening the *Tillage* and encreafing the *Pafture*; which is a conftant detriment to the *Impropriator*. This *partial Inclofure* therefore fhould never be fuffer'd without a general agreement to do the *whole*.

Article XXV.

BEcaufe PARKS are liable to great Abufes and Loffes for want of *Honefty* and due Care, a Steward fhould have a watchful Eye, to fee that the *Keeper* performs his duty, by keeping the Pales or Walls entire, that the Deer do not * ftray, and fo give occafion of Complaint, or elfe of Violence done them : And alfo, that he be diligent in foddering them in fome dry parts of the Park, not only in froft and fnow, but alfo in a *wet feafon*, at which time they want it almoft as much as in harder weather, chiefly to prevent the *Rot*; for a negleft in this Article has been the occafion of the Ruin of many a Park.

THE Park-keeper fhould alfo contrive, in *hard weather*, to beat down the *Haws*, which are a great *delicacy* and nourifhment to the Deer; for it is obferv'd, that they will

---

* I am forry to fay that too many Lardlords (who are fond of out-lying Deer) are carelefs in this affair, and don't confider the Great Damage done to the induftrious Tenant, by not keeping the Deer from the Tenant's Corn, &c. and alfo the great damage done to the young Woods kept in hand.

eagerly

eagerly follow the Perſon who beats 'em down, from one Thorn-pollard to another, in order to *lick* them up, and feed upon them. I have ſeen this practiſ'd with a great deal of pleaſure, and have often wonder'd it is ſo much omitted in moſt Noblemen's Parks. Since therefore this method is found to anſwer both *pleaſure* and *profit*, it is very adviſable that the Steward ſhould preſerve and propagate theſe *White-thorn* Pollards. The ſame might be ſaid with reſpect to the planting the true * *Cheſnuts*, which, after a few years, are apt to bear great quantities of Fruit, which the Deer are *ſtrangely* fond of; and it is obſerv'd, they will very readily *ſhell* the Fruit from its prickly Husk or outward Coat.

MOREOVER, in the management of a Park it ſhould not be forgot always to preſerve a ſufficient number of *male Deer*, gelt at about a year old, one under another; by which means they will be fat at five years old the latter end of *September*, in *rutting* time, when the other Bucks are out of ſeaſon. Theſe *male Deer*, ſo order'd, are call'd HAVIORS, and are accounted a great rarity between Buck and Doe ſeaſons. Neither ſhould the Keeper forget this ſeaſonable piece of wiſdom, (known to be right by all who are nice and curious) *viz.* to order the Skin of the Deer to be got off the very *minute*, if it is poſſible, after he's ſhot; which not only cauſes the Veniſon to have a *richer* taſte, but is a means to preſerve it and keep it ſweet much the longer: A Circumſtance to be much regarded by thoſe who have frequent occaſions to ſend them at a diſtance in hot weather.

---

* This method of propagating White-thorn Pollard and Cheſnuts has been found to ſave not a little Fodder in the Winter.

UNDER

UNDER this Article it may not be amiss to advertise the Steward to see (as much as in him lieth) that the Park-keepers do not abuse the trust repos'd in them by killing too many of the female Fawns at the time when the Does drop them; for the number of these preserv'd should be nearly the same with the number of Does intended to be kill'd in the Winter season: And no less care should be taken that the Keeper (for the *lucre* of Gain both in the Fawns and their Skins) do not suffer them to live too long; for indeed the proper number should be kill'd as soon as possible after the Does have dropt them, lest by sucking too long, the Does have not time to gather Fat a-gainst the Winter season.

IT is also advisable that the Steward should be careful every year to see that the Park be *drove*; *i. e.* that he take an exact account of the number of male and female Deer, entering them down in a Book kept for that purpose, ex-pressing how many Fawns, male and female, there are re-serv'd, as well as the number of both kinds, from one year old to five, together with the number of Bucks and Does kill'd each year. The doing of this (and to a faithful dili-gent Servant it is not much work, especially where the Parks are small) will not a little recommend the Steward's di i-gence, and will at the same time be a great satisfaction to his Lord, to see whether, or how much, his Park every year encreases or decreases: And this Knowledge will be a con-stant Cheque upon the Keepers, that they do not dare to abuse their Trust.

An

An Example of the Method of keeping a Book for this, is as followeth.

Years when the Park was drove.	Fawns 1 year old.		2 years old.		3 years old.		4 years old.		5 years old.		Total Number of Deer.	No kill'd each year	
	males.	females	Males or Prickets	Fe-males.	Males, or Sorels	Fe-males.	Males, or Sores.	Fe-males.	Bucks.	Does.		Bucks.	Does.
Anno													
1724	172	168	147	139	130	127	139	138	210	195	1565	86	48
1725	182	190	159	128	140	120	148	170	225	170	1632	80	40
1726	195	170	149	135	160	134	170	160	240	165	1658	70	35
1727	183	148	153	148	170	130	180	165	247	179	1703	76	30

IF Order and Accuracy in this affair be intended, the Park ought to be divided into two other parts; the *first* of which should serve to drive a small Herd into, in order to be told over exactly; and the *second* part, to keep those told together till the whole is taken an account of.

S   *Arti-*

Article XXVI.

BEcaufe the WOODS belonging to fome Noblemen's Eftates are fo confiderable and valuable a part of them, it would not be prudent to let the whole care and profit of them depend folely upon the Honefty and Care of the *Wood-keeper* ; and therefore *here alfo* will be expected a little watchfulnefs and diligence in a Steward, to fee that the Keeper performs his Duty in the following particulars :

(1.) That he doth keep and preferve the Fences, whether Pales or Hedges, in fuch a manner that no Cattle may be able to get into the Woods, whereby great and incredible mifchief would quickly be done, efpecially among the young Underwoods newly fprung out, of which moft forts of Cattle are very greedy : Wherefore a conftant Care in this Article will be a great means to accelerate their growth and encreafe ; whereas, on the contrary, the Time for the repeated Sale of fuch Woods, by Indolence and Neglect, will be (according to conftant Experience) poftpon'd and retarded, to the great lofs and damage of the Lord.

(2.) That the Keeper do clear off all the Trumpery that grow and cleave to the Timber-trees, efpecially Ivy, which being a Robber and Sucker, much retards their Growth and Encreafe.

(3.) If

(3.) If by the force of Winds any of the larger branches happen to be broken off, that care be taken to cut the remaining part within a few inches of the body of the Tree, flopewife and fmooth, the better to caft off the wet, left it get into the body of the Tree, which in time would corrupt it, either in whole or in part.

(4.) Great care fhould be alfo taken, when Underwoods are to be cut for fale, that the Workmen do not *haggle* them at the place of amputation; neither fhould they be cut too clofe to the ground, rather four or five inches from it, with a fharp Tool flopewife, and the ftroke of the Hatchet *upward*, fo as to leave the furface fmooth, and not fplit, the better to caft off the wet, and to preferve them from rotting.

IT is the Cuftom in many parts of the North, not to cut their Underwoods till they have grown Thirty or Forty Years; but that Cuftom is by no means for the Owner's Intereft; becaufe, upon long Obfervation and Experience, I cannot find that the laft Ten or Fifteen Years anfwers fo well as a quicker return of only † Twenty or Twenty-five years growth; which yet, if care and diligence hath been us'd, fufficiently anfwers all the Ends and Purpofes of thofe who purchafe them.

AFTER Twenty or Twenty-five years growth therefore, when a fale of Wood is determin'd, the firft thing a Steward hath to do, is to have the Lands exactly furvey'd, plotted, and laid out into Acres *parallel* to one another, taking care to view every Acre diftinctly and throughly, in order to confider the Ufes every part of the faid Acre may be apply'd to. For inftance; if there be any fine, tall,

---

† Underwoods above Twenty years growth pays no Tythe.

ftreight *Afh's*, they will turn to the beft account for Coopers ufe : The *Hazles* in the North, and where Coals are found, are profitably imploy'd to make Baskets for the Coal-trade: The *Oak* is ufeful for Spars for ordinary Buildings, and alfo for Pofts and Rails, for Fences and Hedges to preferve the young Quicks, *&c.* It is obfervable, that the Underwoods in the North run moftly upon *Oak*, which is by much the beft, and brings moft profit, by reafon of the Bark, fo ufeful to the Tanners; for tho' there may be fuppos'd to be about an eighth part of *Afh* and other foft Wood intermix'd, yet the Bark of the Underwood that runs chiefly upon *Oak*, commonly fells for half the value of the Underwood.

T H E beft method a Steward can take to guide himfelf in felling Timber and Underwood, and to know the Market-price, is to be well inform'd how the neighbouring Gentlemen fell theirs, always allowing for a difference in Goodnefs; as fuch there will be, on account either of the Sort of the Wood, or of the Nature of the Soil and Situation, or of the accidental misfortunes that have attended it during its time of growth : The Steward muft therefore (as I faid before) ufe that noble Rule of COMPARISON, which if rightly and difcreetly apply'd, will be of no fmall advantage to him, in this part, as well as moft of his other Country affairs.

MOREOVER, a Steward, at his firft entering into bufinefs, fhould take an exact * account of every *fingle* Timber-

---

* The following Account and Table has given greater fatisfaction than the common method ufed by fome Surveyors, who pretend to a Nicety by inferting each Timber-tree in their Map, which is not practicable, except in *very* fmall Farms, and where the Scale is *very* large. I would defire fuch Surveyors to confider how the Map will be defac'd by altering of it when fuch Timber-trees are cut down and fold. Therefore the following Table anfwers much the beft, by reafon the Dimenfions and *Value* are there given. This method puts Noblemen and Gentlemen to lefs Expence, becaufe the other is very tedious, to put each Tree in its proper place; and I fuppofe the cuftom was brought up by fuch as wanted to fpin out Time, and to be paid accordingly.

tree

tree, as well as others likely to become Timber, in all the Woods within his Lord s Manors : And in doing this with advantage, and to purpose, he should have a Book ruled with proper Columns, in order (1.) to insert the fourth part of the Girt of each Tree in inches ; (2.) the Length of each Tree in Feet ; (3) the number of solid Feet in each Tree ; (4) the value *per* Foot that each Tree is worth according to its Dimensions and Goodness ; (5) the value of the *Body* of each Tree, in proportion to the aforesaid Price ; (6) the value of the *Head* of each Tree ; (7) the value of the *Bark* of each Oak-tree, which generally holds to be about a third part of the value of the Body and Head ; and (lastly) a Column for the value of the Body, the Head, and Bark added together ; an Example whereof is exhibited in a following Page.

AND it may be observ'd, that a Book put into this method will not fail to give great Satisfaction to his Lord, who hath now something to depend upon, whenever his Necessities or his Inclinations call for a *certain* Sum of Money. However, after such Sale, the Book must be alter'd, and such Trees struck out of it.

IT should also be remember'd that, when an Account is taken of the several Timber-trees, they be mark'd with Iron-stamps made on purpose : Only before the Stamp is apply'd, the rough part of the Bark should be taken off with a Hatchet, that the Impression may be made easie and visible : And, to make it *lasting*, the Stamp should not go deeper than the Bark, because in such case the number will soon grow up ; but otherwise it may last several years by renewing, which is no undesirable Circumstance.

T

To treat of the beſt methods of cultivating and dreſ-
ſing all ſorts of Timber-trees, ſo as beſt and ſooneſt to
anſwer the End of the Planter, would carry me beyond
the limits of this intended ſhoit Eſſay ; and it may better
be deferred to a Treatiſe of Husbandry, as practis'd in
ſeveral parts of the Kingdom, of which I have already
given the Publick notice, and which I intend (GOD willing) to finiſh in due time : However, before I leave this
Article, I would adviſe every Steward throughly to conſider the beſt Advantage that even the worſt of Land may
be turn'd to.   For inſtance ;   On my Surveys I have
ſeen, to my great ſurprize, a great number of Acres,
(not capable of being drain'd, except by a Sum of Money by no means equal to the profit) lain quite waſte ;
whereas *Willows* and Oziers planted *very* thick would, even
in the moiſteſt Bogs, grow and bear good Lop, and by
their encreaſe make a good return of Rent, by reaſon
of the great and conſtant demand for them, chiefly on
the account of Baskets for the Coal-trade, and for many
other Uſes.

IT may not be amiſs in this Article to ſhew the Uſe
of the Table of Timber-meaſure (which is placed at the
end of *The Duty of a Steward*) ready caſt up, from 3 inches
ſquare to 75 ; and from 1 foot to 45 in length.

FIRST gird the Tree with a String about the middle,
then double the String twice, which is call'd a fourth part
of the Girt, which you muſt exactly meaſure upon your
Rule ; as, ſuppoſe it is 19 inches, a method that reduces
round Timber to ſquare the cuſtomary way; but if the
Tree is full grown with a thick Bark, it muſt be call'd but
18 in-

18 inches, whereas in others half an inch is sufficient, as every Practitioner will easily judge: Then measure the height of the Tree by the help of a Ladder and a long Pole, and suppose it to be 36 foot high; look then in the Table for 18 inches at the top, and cast your Eye downwards to 36 foot length, and at the angle of meeting you'll find just 81 foot for the number of solid feet which the Tree contains: And so the same for any other number. *NB.* The parts of a foot for the Content is given in tenths, which is nearer than the Dimensions can be taken.

THERE hath been great pains taken by several Authors upon this Subject, endeavouring to set aside this customary way of measuring, which indeed (strictly speaking) is false, and gives the Content in feet above a fifth part too little; but since a customary price is settled accordingly, it is but a *vain* and *fruitless* Attempt; because if the one is alter'd, the other must be alter'd also, which comes to the same thing.

NB. IT may not be amiss to observe under this *Article*, that it sometimes happens, in a sale of Underwood, that the Persons who buy it cannot lead the whole off the premises before the latter end of the Summer, when the new Shoots are got to a considerable height: But this, if possible, should be avoided; because the treading of the Horses, and the impression of the Waggon-wheels, do a great deal of damage to the young Springs: However, to prevent as much mischief as may be, the Steward should see that the Wain-Horses and Oxen be *muzzled*, to prevent their *cropping* the young Springs, which they

are

are very fond of, whereby the Underwood hath often
ſuſtain'd incredible damage.

I<small>T</small> hath been often the wonder of an Agent, who
hath been ſent down to view and value the Woods, why
they were not ſo good as thoſe of the neighbouring Gentlemen reſiding in the Country, at the ſame number of
years growth. The Anſwer to which is obvious : The
Gentlemen take care to prevent the miſchief above, and
the Steward, either by *Abſence* or *Indolence* or *Neglect*,
ſuffers it ; and ſometimes alſo, for a ⁂ *valuable* Conſideration, connives at the turning of the Woodward's and Tenants Cattle into the young Springs ; which, to my knowledge, in a few years has done at leaſt a Hundred pound
damage in a Wood of Eight or Nine hundred pound
value.

  ⁂ I know of ſeveral Inſtances where Woodwards have rais'd a great deal
of Money in breeding up young Cattle in the Woods and young Springs ;
but when the Nobleman came down to look into his Affairs, he ſoon put a
ſtop to it, by diſcharging both Steward and Woodward.

A par-

A particular Account of the Number of OAK *Timber-Trees, and such others as are likely to be Timber, in* SKITSCREW-WOOD.

Number of the Trees	The 4th part of the Girt of each Tree in inches.	The length of each Tree in feet	Number of solid Feet in each Tree.	Value *per* foot of the several Trees.		Value of the Body of each Tree.			Value of the Head of each Tree.			Value of the Bark of each Tree, which is commonly about a third of the Head and Body.			Total Value of each Tree.		
				s.	*d.*	*l.*	*s.*	*d.*	*l.*	*s.*	*d.*	*l.*	*s.*	*d.*	*l.*	*s.*	*d.*
1	15	25	39	1 :	4	2	12	0	0	4	6	0	18	10	3	15	4
2	11	22	18½	1 :	2	1	1	7	0	1	6	0	7	8	1	10	9
3	12	23	23	1 :	4	1	10	8	0	2	6	0	11	1	2	4	3
4	11½	27	25	1 :	2	1	9	2	0	2	0	0	10	5	2	1	7
5	11½	19	17½	1 :	3	1	1	10	0	2	6	0	8	1	1	12	5
6	9½	25	15½	1 :	2	0	18	1	0	1	0	0	6	4	1	5	5
7	15	25	39	1 :	6	2	18	6	0	3	0	1	0	6	4	2	0
8	12	23	23	1 :	4	1	10	8	0	2	6	0	11	1	2	4	3
9	15	17	26½	1 :	2	1	10	11	0	3	6	0	11	6	2	5	11
10	11	25	21	1 :	4	1	8	0	0	2	6	0	10	2	2	0	8
11	13	29	34	1 :	4	2	5	4	0	4	6	0	16	7	3	6	5
12	12½	24	26	1 :	6	1	19	0	0	3	0	0	14	0	2	16	0
13	13	24	28	1 :	6	2	2	0	0	3	6	0	15	2	3	0	8
14	13	38	44½	1 :	6	3	6	9	0	3	0	1	3	3	4	13	0
15	13	23	27	1 :	2	1	11	6	0	3	0	0	11	6	2	6	0
16	12	23	23	1 :	3	1	8	9	0	3	6	0	10	9	2	3	0
17	11½	25	23	1 :	0	1	3	0	0	2	0	0	8	4	1	13	0
18	9½	24	15	1 :	00	0	15	0	0	1	6	0	5	6	1	2	0
19	11½	20	18	1 :	2	1	1	0	0	4	6	0	8	6	1	14	0
20	11½	27	24½	1 :	2	1	8	7	0	3	0	0	10	6	2	2	1
21	10½	27	20½	1 :	2	1	3	11	0	2	0	0	8	8	1	14	7
22	14½	23	33½	1 :	6	2	10	3	0	4	0	0	18	1	3	12	4
23	15½	32	53	1 :	6	3	19	6	0	4	0	1	7	10	5	11	4
24	15	24	37½	1 :	6	2	16	3	0	5	0	1	0	7	4	2	4
Total			655½			43	11	3	3	12	6	16	4	11	62	19	4

U *Arti-*

Article XXVII.

IN the 'foregoing Article I have hinted how Lands that are ſubject to Wet, are boggy, and cannot eaſily be drain'd without great charge, may be improv'd ; yet nevertheleſs, where Drains can be made at a tolerable charge, it is adviſeable to ſet about it, eſpecially if it ſo happens that the ſame paſſage that brings it in from Rivers and Brooks may alſo carry it off. The Improvement of Land by *floating* with muddy Water is now pretty well underſtood, and frequently practis'd : But yet there are many Inſtances of low boggy Lands, that are ſuffer'd to lie under Water half the Year, by which means they are ſtarv'd, and worth little ; which yet, with ſome expence in making frequent and deep Drains, might be made to have a communication with the neighbouring Brooks and Rivers, whereby they will receive *vaſt* Improvements, even to three times the former value : For as theſe Drains will occaſionally bring up the muddy water to enrich the Land, ſo they will carry the water back when it is clear.

BUT before a Steward begins this Work, he muſt by the help of a *Spirit-Level* find out whether the River or Brook is higher or lower than the Lands on each ſide, and how much. In the next place, he muſt level all the

other

other parts, in order to find where the Water can be carried off at pleasure : After which, by the help of Sluices placed in the feveral parts of the feveral Trenches, each part may eafily be flooded, and fo the muddy water may be continued, and convey'd from one part to another. I have known Inftances of low Lands lying near a Market-Town frequented by *Tanners*, the very Liquor of whofe *Tann-vats*, being made to find its way into the low Grounds, hath ftrangely enrich'd them : And it hardly need be faid, that if their Refufe-Bark be alfo fuperinduced, no greater Riches can well be defir'd.

Article XXVIII.

I Have known great Improvements made on large and extended parcels of Land lying uninclos'd, and on a warm Soil well fhelter'd with Trees and Hills, by having *moveable* Hurdles, or Pofts and Rails; by which means the Cattle were mov'd from one *frefh* Pafture to another, and by which management more Cattle were kept, and thofe better fed ; for as a fucceffion of *frefh* Food gave them better nourifhment, fo they were conftantly obferv'd to be fat much the fooner. This is taken notice of as an Advertifement to the Steward, that in cafe large Parks and Forefts happen to be kept in hand for his Lord's ufe,

he

he may have regard to it, as a thing that will turn to good advantage with a little charge : And by this means his Lord may have his Beef and Mutton sent up alive to *London*, at a cheaper rate than to go to Market. And, to do this to the best advantage, the Steward should be advis'd to stock the Ground with *Scotch Keylys* or *Welch Runts* at Midsummer *half-fat*, that they may be *made up*, and their Improvement compleated, before the hard weather comes on; for if they are bought in *lean*, or later, they will, in the Graziers phrase, *eat off their Heads* with * Hay in the Winter. The *Sheep* proper to be bought in for such Lands are those fetch'd from *Norfolk*, or some other distant barren Country : But it is to be remember'd, that Care be taken that they be not immediately put into the best *Park-Land*, but rather into some *Fallows*, or ordinary breeding Pastures, for about a week before they are put into the *best*, where they are to be made fat : Not forgetting also a piece of excellent and seasonable Advice, given by a † skilful and experienc'd Grazier, To bleed them in the Vein just under their Eye, a day after they come off their Journey. A neglect of these two material points relating to Sheep, has been observ'd to be the occasion of several Distempers amongst them, some of which have ended in their Death soon after.

Upon the whole, it is very adviseable for all Noblemen and Gentlemen, whose Estates are not too far from *London*, to keep Lands in hand to the value of Three or

---

* If Noblemen or Gentlemen are desirous to have, this curious sort of Beef sent up to *London*, &c. all the Year round, then provisions for Hay or Rye-flower must be made in the Winter accordingly. [See the Appendix.]

† The famous Merchant *Morley*.

Four

Four hundred a year, more or lefs; not only to fup-
ply them with Neceffaries whilft they are in the Country, but in *London* alfo; which, if manag'd by the Steward
abroad, and by the Dairy-woman at home, to the *beft* advantage, may be made to anfwer, and to turn to a very
good account, by having almoft every thing fent up to
London in feafon, and at the *beft* hand. This is not a
matter of *Theory* only; but I have known feveral Inftances of thofe who are reckon'd the beft *Oeconomifts*, who
have practis'd it with great Satisfaction, and, as they
find it to anfwer their End, are refolv'd to continue the
practice.

BUT as the Succefs of this whole Affair is owing to
the Steward's *Skill* in Husbandry, fo that Knowledge is
here taken for granted; and his Lord will have ftill a
more *feeling* Senfe of it, when he comes to find that the
Steward is able to direct a Tenant, upon occafion, to
manage his Farm, or even his *Whole* Eftate, to the beft
advantage.

X   *Arti-*

Article XXIX.

IN a Country where Slate and Tyle and Lime are not *extreamly* dear, a Steward fhould ufe his beft Endeavours to oblige all his Lord's Tenants to cover their Houfes with Slate or Tile, not only as a better Security againft Accidents and the Misfortune of † Fire, but alfo as it prevents that great confumption of Straw, the conftant Demand for Thatch and Covering, too much ufed in moft Country Villages, *robbing* the Land of fuch quantities of Manure; which is felt very *feverely* in fuch places, and on fuch Farms, where little elfe is to be got but what the Premifes afford. This Advice of the Steward fhould alfo extend it felf to the Freehold Tenants round about, that they may be made fenfible how much it is for their own, as well as their Country's Good.

---

† The dreadful Fire which happen'd at *Thropfton* in *Northampton-fhire*, and feveral others, have chiefly been encreas'd by the *multitude* of *Thatch'd* Houfes.

Arti-

Article XXX.

A Steward, when he draws out proper Covenants, to oblige Tenants to keep up their Farms in a due course of Husbandry, should not forget this material one, viz. *Not to commit Waste in any sort*, and especially by erecting Brick-kilns, and by digging Clay in order to make Bricks for sale, without giving a *valuable* Consideration for the same. This I have found practis'd, to the great Injury of some of the best Land; and the whole has been kept a Secret from the Lord. Nay, for want of such a Covenant, I have known that the Freehold Tenants have pared the Turf off from extraordinary good Land, and carried the rich Mould for eight or ten inches deep away, in order to improve *their own* Lands, laying the Turf down again : And when they have committed this *Waste*, I have known the Land thrown up into the Lord's hand, to make the best of it.

Arti-

Article XXXI.

IN letting Pasture-Lands to such Tenants as breed or have a *great* stock of *Horses*, some Caution should be used, that the *best* Land be not allotted for such purposes; forasmuch as a constant feeding with such Cattle only, is known to breed coarse sowre Grass, and in time, greatly to hurt and much *diminish* the Value of such Land. And indeed, where-ever Horses feed, there should be an allowance of considerable *Superinductions* every year, of all such Dungs and Manures as the Country affords.

Article XXXII.

A Steward, upon his Surveys, should observe whether the Tenants keep the Bye-roads leading thro' their Grounds in good repair, especially the Gate-ways and Bridges; for want of which great damage hath been done by Travellers breaking the Hedges, and riding over good Land on each side the way. It would be too much beside

my

my prefent purpofe to direct the beft method for mending Roads ; and it may perhaps hereafter be done by one who has promis'd it : But it may not be amifs here to obferve, that the great myftery of making Roads good, is to lay and keep them *dry* ; for which purpofe they fhould ever lie *round* and *high* in the middle, which may be eafily fo order'd, by throwing on what comes out of the Ditches into the middle, and afterwards, when the Earth is well fettled, at Midfummer, the beft Gravel, Stones, or Rubbifh which the Country affords fhould be laid upon it. When this hath been done with Judgment and Skill, even thofe Roads which (by means of ftagnating water) have been almoft unpaffable at Midfummer, have become fit for a galloping Horfe in the winter.

Article XXXIII.

THERE is a great deal of Difcretion, as well as Judgment, to be ufed by a Steward when he enters upon that *difficult* work of letting his Lord's Farms, efpecially if he finds there is a good deal of reafon for raifing the Rents : But becaufe there is one Circumftance which I think may tend to miflead him, I fhall here advertife him never to parcel out Lands to *fmall* Freeholders in Townfhips where there are large Commons without STINT, tho' they would give (as fometimes they will offer) double the

value

value of what the Land is really worth to a large Farm ; which would prove in the end a manifest prejudice to the Lord's Tenants, because those small Freeholders only make use of those Lands rented *dear* to put their Cattle into at such times as the Commons are under water, or in the winter, when 'tis so cold and open that the Cattle are ready to starve. By which it may appear, that a Freeholder who hath only an House and Homested of Twenty shillings a year, may improve it to Ten pounds a year, or more : But then, by such a Contrivance, the Commons would be so full stock'd, that the Lord's Tenants, who rent large Farms, would not receive their proportion of Advantage, which was one motive that put them upon taking their Farms : So that the Steward's well-intended Aim of getting an advanced Rent, hath prov'd in the end a real Hindrance to the Improvement of the whole.

THUS again, in other *Townships*, where 'tis the Custom to STINT the Commons and Common-Fields, the Steward should take care that the Richer Tenants do not *stock* them beyond the Custom of the Manor. This is what I have too often found abused to a *very great* degree, to the no small damage of the poorer Tenants, who are not always in a condition to buy such a Stock as is their due to put in. In such cases the Steward should oblige the Richer Tenants not to put in beyond their STINT, without making an Allowance to the poorer sort for the Sheep, &c. that they put in above their number in their stead ; and by no means to suffer the whole to be overstockt. These Abuses used formerly to be *strictly* observ'd at the Court-BARON, but of late years have been little

regarded,

regarded, except in fome Manors, where the diligent *Steward* would *exert* himfelf, by *prefenting* them that had offended; and the more when he found the fubftantial Tenants had agreed together not to *prefent* one another, and to *crufh* thofe poorer Tenants that fhould offer to do it.

Article XXXIV.

A Steward, before he lets any confiderable Farm to a feeming-good advantage of an advanc'd rent, fhould be well fatisfied of the *Ability* of the Tenant; for want of which he manifeftly, and of courfe, muft run behind-hand, tho' he hath no ill bargain. A Farm of a Hundred pounds a year requires at the leaft Three hundred pounds Stock; and if 'tis a grazing Farm, above Four hundred pounds. The want of fuch a fubftance either forces them to be content to *breed* upon fuch *good* Land as would make their Cattle fat, or elfe to take in *Joifts* at any rate they can get, till they can raife a Stock of their own : Which is a method that often proves the ruin of a Tenant, except he has the good fortune to rent a Farm at half the value.

THE like may be faid when a Tenant firft enters up-on his Farm, that he ftocks it with Cattle fuitable to the nature of the Land : Pafture and Meadow Grounds in the

Nor-

Northern parts of *England*, worth about Twenty or Twenty-
five fhillings an Acre, fhould be ftock'd with the beft and
largeft Cattle; the middling Pafture or Meadow, worth
about Ten or Twelve fhillings an Acre, with a leffer fize;
and the more barren, with the fmaller fort, chiefly for
Breeding, in order to be fold off to better Land to be
made fat.

Article XXXV.

A S it ought to be the conftant Study and Endeavour of
a Steward to promote the eafe and comfortable fub-
fiftance of his Lord's Tenants, fo in a particular manner
he fhould endeavour to prevent *all* loads and incumbran-
ces upon their honeft Endeavours, fuch efpecially as are
wont to arife from Strangers and Vagrants harbouring
amongft them, fometimes fo long till they or their Chil-
dren obtain fettlements, and when they are difabled or
fuperannuated, demand Relief. And this of confequence
muft be a means, time after time, of encreafing the Poor's
Seffes, and loading the Parifh with a more than ordinary
Tax, *more* fometimes than they are able to bear, which
proves the occafion of A R R E A R S in Rent. Our Laws
have well guarded againft this Evil; but the Indolence
of *Parifhes* (where Every-body's Bufinefs is No-body's)
is commonly fo great, that little or no Care is taken in
this

this affair : Wherefore the *Steward's Care* and Vigilance are the more neceffary to put the Laws in execution, and to have recourfe to Juftice, to prevent the mifchief and Burthen which, in the end, would otherwife fall upon the Lord of the Manor.

UNDER this Article it is alfo proper to obferve, that a Steward, in order to prevent Law-fuits, unneceffary Expences, and lofs of Time, fhould endeavour (as much as in him lieth) to act as a *Mediator* between one Tenant and another, when they happen to quarrel and difpute about *Trifles*; or indeed in any other affair, where any real Difficulty arifes about Property. The Ufefulnefs of this Office of a Steward is fo apparent, that I need not paint it in any other or more words.

AND altho' poffibly there might be other and further enlargements made on the Office and Duty of a Steward, yet forafmuch as I apprehend I have touch'd upon the moft neceffary and moft material Parts of the Office; and as I intend to avoid *prolixity* in repeating any Apology which the Freedom I have ufed might be fuppos'd to want; I fhall, in this and the next Article, conclude this Part of my Treatife by perfwading *Stewards*, and others, to obferve and practife fome fuch following rational method of *Jurveying* and drawing up the Particulars of Eftates, before they begin to make *Improvements* from the old rents, that each Tenant's Farm may be fettled in a due *proportion* of Rent, and that they may keep their Accompts fo, as to diftinguifh the feveral *kinds* of *Articles* feparately made; which will prove no fmall Satisfaction to their Lord.

Z   THE

THE following Accompts are intended to be in great meafure Examples; but the Steward is to take notice, that 'tis his Duty to bring what was formerly a Perquifite (*i. e.* every thing which the Eftate produceth) to Accompt, and to content himfelf with a handfom Salary, which I am perfwaded, both from their own Inclination, and from what hath been here faid, *moft* Noblemen will think it their *Intereft* to allow.

Article XXXVI.

AS a Steward fhould know the Quantity and Quality of every parcel of Land occupied by the feveral Tenants, fo likewife he fhould have a *Map* of the whole drawn out in the moft perfect Method ; which may fhew not only the Quantity, but alfo the true figure of every parcel, by reprefenting all the bends in the Hedges, or other boundaries thereof, fo nearly, that he may detect any Tenant from alienating the leaft part of any parcel from his Lord ; and alfo may be able to convince his Lord thereof. And he will alfo (by feeing in the *Map* the pofition every parcel in the Eftate has with refpect to one another) be able to judge (on the demife of any of thofe Tenants that rent any of the fmall Farms) what parcels are proper to lay to one Farm, and what to another ; and
alfo

alfo what convenient alterations may be made in any of the Farms at any time. And here it may be proper to propofe to the Surveyor of a Manor, or Nobleman's Eftate, the moft perfect Method now ufed to take fuch a *Survey*, whereby with care he may do his work fo correct, that it may anfwer the abovemention'd End, which the common methods will not : And, in the firft place, he fhould provide himfelf with a good THEODOLITE, well graduated, with a *Telefcope* thereto, and alfo a *Spirit-Level*, and the whole to be fo well fixt together, that there be no fhake in it, on turning round the *Index* in taking an Angle therewith.

AND now it may be neceffary to give a Defcription of one of the beft fort of THEODOLITES ever yet invented, for the ufe of a Surveyor in meafuring and mapping a Manor or Nobleman's Eftate, made by Mr. JONATHAN SISSON, at the corner of *Beauford* Buildings in the *Strand* (a Figure whereof is in the Map fronting the Title Page of the Book.) The Ball and Socket of this Inftrument are fo contriv'd, that by the help of four Screws placed at right Angles to one another from the Centre, the whole is very readily fixt *horizontal*, and firm from any motion on moving the Index, there being a double *Sextant* of equal *Radius* to the Limb (with a *Spirit-Level* fixt in it, and a *Telefcope* above it) that moves in a Circle at right Angles to the *Index* on the Limb, whereby the *Vertical* Angles may be taken as readily as the *horizontal*, and at the fame time ; and fo the *hypothenufal* lines may be reduced to *horizontal*, which are thofe that fhould always be laid down in plotting any Survey : And the Head of the three-legg'd Staff is of brafs, and not liable to fhake like
the

the wooden ones : The Needle in the Compaſs-box hangs on a Pin of temper'd Steel (turn'd and poliſh'd in a Lath) on which it moves very freely ; and the Limb is ſo curiouſly divided, that tho' there be three *Indexes* at 120° from one another, with *Nonus's* Diviſions on each, to ſhew the Decimal parts of a Degree, yet you ſhall perceive no inequality in the Diviſions on any part of the whole Circle : And there is a Spring and Screw to the Index, under the Teleſcope, to fix it to any part of the Limb. The whole is well Framed, very portable, and well contriv'd for diſpatch of buſineſs.

AND now, if the Surveyor with one of theſe *Theodolites* enters on a ſurvey, his beſt way will be, at his firſt ſtation (after having fixt it *horizontal*) to place his *Index* at 360 on the Limb, and alſo his *Needle* at the ſame in the Compaſs-box, and then to take the *Angle* of the firſt Line on the Limb, which will be the ſame with the Needle ; which having ſet down in his Field-book, then let him do the ſame with his ſecond Line, and there fix the Index to the Limb ; and then his *Theodolite* may be carried to his ſecond ſtation, where having fixt it *horizontal*, he muſt turn the whole Limb about till the *Vertical* hair in the Teleſcope cuts the Object left at his firſt ſtation ; then looſening the Index-ſcrew, he muſt turn the Index till the ſame hair in his Teleſcope cuts the Object for his third ſtation, and then he muſt fix the Index as before : And if he thus proceeds on to never ſo many Stations, he will always find that either one end or the other of his Needle will correſpond with the Index, ſo near as to detect all *Errors* that may happen in ſetting down the Angles taken on the Limb : And by this method (on his plotting the Survey) he may

set

set off as many Angles as he pleafes at once, laying down his Protractor (which fhould be a circular one, well graduated, and at leaft fix inches diameter) by which his *ftationary* Lines may be much *exacter* laid down, than by fetting off each fucceffive Angle from each Line drawn by the preceeding Angle; which is the way in common ufe by almoft all Surveyors. Now, if by this method the Surveyor will go round the plot to be furvey'd, and will take all the Angles, as well as meafure all the ftationary Lines, if the fum of thofe lines doth not exceed four miles, then a miftake made of one Chain in any one of the ftationary lines may be difcover'd, if he is careful in fetting off the Angles, and the lengths of his ftationary lines; and, that it is not done by a fmaller *Scale* than four of *Gunter*'s Chains to an Inch: Therefore this way, with care, the Surveyor may be fure of not making any material Error; but by thofe ufed by the moft noted Surveyors, they are not fure they are within One Acre in Forty, if they have made no miftake in their meafur'd lines; and if they have made fuch, they often don't know it; by which they may in fome places err more than after the rate of One in Twenty, without miftrufting any Error at all. As for the common *Theodolites* made with plain Sights only, and no *Telefcope* and *Spirit-Level*, but which have wooden heads at the top of the three-legg'd Staff, they cannot be depended on in going round a large furvey; for, with plain fights, your Eye not being fixt (as it muft be allow'd the Image of an Object is in a Telefcope) whatever your Eye varies from the true line clofe by, is encreas'd at a diftance in proportion to the length thereof, fo that an Angle can't be furely taken within a few minutes, tho' the *Theodolite* fhould happen to be fixt *horizontal*; but, without a *Spirit-*

Level,

Level, the fixing it so can only be guess'd at ; and where the ground is hilly, and most wanted to be so, you can't be sure of being within two or three degrees ; by which I shall demonstrate, the Surveyor is liable to a very great *Error* : As for any *Error* by the wooden Head's shaking, or motion of the Ball in the Socket on turning round the Index, yet if it be turn'd quite round to the Object it was mov'd from, it may be seen if the Limb has mov'd ; and thus, by new turning the Index, an Error may be rectified ; but very few Surveyors will allow themselves that Time, and therefore should have one that don't need it.   As for all large Surveys done by the *plain Table,* they ought not to be depended on, but should be done *anew* ; for this Instrument, besides all the inconveniency attending common *Theodolites,* is subject to many others, for with these there is no remedy if the Table alters by moving the Index, without drawing new lines by the erroneous ones, which will cause confusion ; also the Paper will extend, or shrink up, as the *Weather* alters to moist or dry, by which the stationary lines will be *encreas'd* or *lessen'd* : And besides, a Surveyor will not stand about the exactness necessary in the stationary lines, in the open Field, when his Assistants or others are by him, and especially in sharp cold weather, as he would do in a warm Room by himself : And then if, on coming round to the place he began at, he finds his work does not close on the point it should do, (which in a large Quantity is not to be expected by this Instrument any thing near) he must either alter the Angle or Length of the last line, or both, to make it close, (*i. e.* the end of the last line to touch the beginning of the first) to conceal the Error from any body near ; for if he discovers it, and no Error is found in the measur'd lines,

lines, his Inſtrument or Judgment muſt be condemn'd, becauſe he can be liable to no material Error in the Angles, but by a real fault or defect in the Inſtrument.

ALSO in the method Surveyors uſe in caſting up the quantity of the Lands they meaſure, they are liable to ſeveral Errors, being oblig'd to form and caſt up as many Triangles as the Field has ſides, abating two, which in ſome irregular Fields are very many; and if halfing the baſe, perpendicular, or product of any of them ſhould be forgot, there might infenſibly be a great Error committed, or one of the many little Triangles might be forgot; ſo an Error may be that way, beſides the Errors in every of thoſe lines that form the Triangles, the ſum total of which in many is not inconſiderable; but theſe Errors are prevented in the Method uſed by my ſelf and Mr. *William Gardiner,* in reducing all irregular figures to *one Triangle,* and in as little time as they can draw the lines that form their Triangles, if they do them as correct; and then we have but one Triangle to caſt up, very nearly equal to the whole Field.

Now, that it is neceſſary the *Theodolite* ſhould be fixt horizontal, may be ſeen by the following Example: Suppoſe you were to meaſure from A to B, which is a ſtreight line, but a hill being between, you could ſee no further than C at the top of the hill, at which place you fix your Theodolite, which ſuppoſe one of the common ſort, with the addition of a Teleſcope to it, but no Spirit-Level, then C being on the edge of the hill, where it is down-hill not only to A and B, but alſo more ſteep to D, it will then be very likely that the plane of the Limb of your *Theodolite* would

would be nearer to the plane of the Superficies of the Ground between C and D than two degrees from the *horizontal* Plane, when you ſhall have fixt it as near as you can to the *horizontal* Plane; but allowing it to be juſt two degrees, then ſuppoſe you fix your *Index* at 360, and direct your Teleſcope down to A, to do which you depreſs it ten degrees, then you turn it to look at B, where it is ſtill depreſs'd ten degrees; I ſay then, in this caſe, your Index will cut 179° : 18' : 38″ very nearly; for A by calculation is taken 20' : 41″ out of its true place on one ſide, and B is the ſame on the other ſide, which together (the whole being thrown upon B) puts B 41' : 22″ out of its true place, which is full twelve Links, if but ten Chains from C to B; and if twenty Chains, it will be double, *viz.* twenty-four Links. Now this is better than can be depended on in ſuch a caſe without a Spirit-Level, but without a *Teleſcope* you may be liable to near double this Error in this Caſe, and to the ſame Error nearly in any Caſe, being you can't know when any Object is cut nearer than to about 20'; and therefore prodigious Errors may be committed by a *plain Table*, whoſe plane on the like occaſion, if there ſhould be any obſervation made at D, (the Surveyor not knowing better) would place the Plane of his *Plain Table* nearer to the Plane of the Superficies of the ground between C and D than two (or even ten) degrees from the horizontal Plane, which laſt wou'd throw B out of its true place 3° : 30' : 27″, which, if B is but ten Chains from C, is near 61¼ Links; and if twenty Chains, it will be but one Chain and 22½ Links nearly out of its true place : And this added to all the other Errors which may be committed by that ABOMI-NABLE Inſtrument, ſhou'd deter *all* Perſons that know it from depending thereon in any Large Survey.

Here

Here follows a Calculation of the Errors in the two
foremention'd Cafes.

(1)   D   (2)

As Rad. to S. √. 10° =Log. 9.2396702
fo is tang. √ 2° — =Log. 8.5430838
to tang. 20′: 41″ nearly Log. 7.7827540

As Rad. to S. √ 10° =Log. 9.2396702
fo is tang. √ 10° —=Log. 9.2463188
to tang. √ 1°-45′-13″⅐=Log. 8.4859890

then

As Rad. to 1000 Links =Log. 3.0000000
fo is S. √ 20′ 41″ nearly Log. 7.7827462
to 6.06382 Links — =Log. 0.7827462

As Rad. to 1000 links =Log. 3.0000000
fo is S. √ 1°-45′-13″⅐=Log. 8.4857856
to 30.6045 Links—=Log. 1.4857856

then 6.06382 being doubled, is
12.12764 Links, being what B
is put out of his true place, when
the Limb of the *Theodolite* is in-
clined but 2° to the horizontal
Plane, and the *Telefcope* deprefs'd
10° below the *Horizon*, and that
A and B are at right Angles to
the greateft declination of the
Plane of the Limb.

then 30.6045 being doubled, is
61.209 Links, being what B is
put out of his true place, when
the *Plain Table* is inclin'd to the
horizontal Plane in an Angle of
10°, and each Object at A and B
depreft 10° below the *Horizon*, and are at right Angles to
the greateft declination of the
Plane of the *Plain Table*.

A   B   C

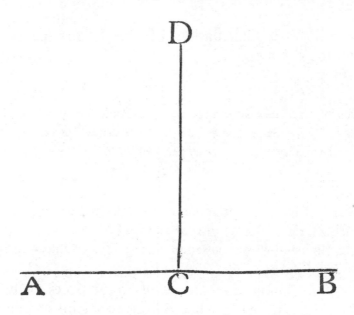

Note, Tho' I approve of the *Needle*, as being of very great ufe, as it is a fure Cheque upon any Error that may be committed thro' miftaking a Number on the Limb, yet is it by no means to be depended upon alone, as too many Surveyors do, by reafon of it's great difpatch ; for we can't be certain it gives every particular Angle true within a few degrees.

A

A
SURVEY
O F

𝕿𝖍𝖊 𝕸𝖆𝖓𝖔𝖗 𝖔𝖋 K———, 𝖎𝖓 𝖙𝖍𝖊 𝕮𝖔𝖚𝖓𝖙𝖞 𝖔𝖋 H———:

CONTAINING

The Particulars of the feveral FARMS following, *now* in the poffeffion of His Grace the Duke of *K*———, Lord of the faid Manor.

Survey'd, *Valued*, and *Improv'd* by EDWARD LAURENCE, Surveyor.

NB. The Defign of drawing up thefe Particulars is, to fhew the neceffity of every Steward or Agent's having a Survey drawn out in this manner following, before he begins to make an Improvement from an *old-rented* Eftate, in order to fettle each Tenant's Farm in a due proportion of Rent ; becaufe it plainly appears by the following Particulars, that the old rents were not fo : And had the Common Method of Poundage been ufed, 'twould have been a means to have prevented fo good an Improvement as has *now* been made in this proper way, to the Tenants fatisfaction, *i. e.* being *equally* ferv'd *all* alike.

THE other fide, oppofite to each Particular, is only Ruled and Titled, in order to enter any Alterations that may happen hereafter in the Farms.

Tenant's Name, and Lands.	Arable inclos'd. a r p	Common Arable. a r p	Pasture. a r p	Meadow. a r p	Total Number of Acres. a r p	Yearly Value per Acre. at s. d.	Yearly value of the several Parcels. l. s. d.
Robert Hunt for the Priory Farm.							
N°. (1) { Old Rent ——— l. s. d. 80 : 0 : 0 / New Rent ——— 105 : 0 : 0 }							
A Messuage, with Barn, Stable, Yard, &c. and Garth adjoyning,	—	—	—	—	—	20 : 0	1 15 6
Priory Closes in two parcels —	—	—	13 7	—	—	18 : 0	22 14 6
Monks Meadow —	—	—	25 1 5	10 1	—	25 : 0	12 17 0
Chantry Croft —	—	—	14 3 15	—	—	15 : 0	11 0 0
Priest Croft —	—	—	9 2 9	—	—	15 : 0	7 3 0
Apple-tree Close —	7 2 11	—	—	—	—	12 : 0	4 11 6
Crabb-tree Close —	9 1 5	—	—	—	—	10 : 0	4 13 0
Castle Close —	—	—	15 0 16	—	—	13 : 0	8 16 6
Castle Ings —	—	—	—	9 0 25	—	25 : 0	11 8 0
Broad Field —	10 0 18	—	—	—	—	8 : 0	4 1 0
The Banks, in three parcels, —	16 2 9	—	—	—	—	6 : 0	5 0 0
The Back of Peal —	—	—	18 3 38	—	—	11 : 0	10 9 0
30 Lands in Thirsk Common-Field, —	—	21 1 30	—	—	—	6 : 0	6 8 6
Total	43 2 3	21 1 30	85 2 10	19 1 32	169 3 35	L.	110 17 6

NB. The whole is Tythe-free.

NB. The abatement of Five pounds a Year less than the value, is in consideration of this Tenant's being oblig'd to divide the larger parcels of the ... into smaller ones, in order to improve them.

Tenants

Tenant's Name, and Lands.	Arable inclos'd.			Common Arable.			Pasture.			Meadow.			Total Number of Acres.			Yearly Value per Acre.	Yearly value of the several Parcels.	
	a	r	p	a	r	p	a	r	p	a	r	p	a	r	p	at	l.	s. d.
Total																		

Cc

Tenant's Name, and Lands.	Arable inclos'd			Common Arable			Pasture			Meadow			Total Number of Acres			Yearly Value per Acre			Yearly value of the several Parcels.		
	a	r	p	a	r	p	a	r	p	a	r	p	a	r	p	l.	s.	d.	l.	s.	d.
Thomas Newton, for Blyth Farm.																					
N° (2) { Old Rent — 68:6:3 / New Rent — 82:0:0																					
A Messuage, with Barns, Stables, Yard, and Homestead adjoyning,							2	3	12				—	—	—		20	0	2	17	0
The Shaws, in two parcels, —	17	3	20										—	—	—		8	0	7	2	6
Cow Clofe —							9	1	0				—	—	—		12	0	5	11	0
Oldby Clofe —							5	1	5				—	—	—		11	0	2	17	10
Kirkhow Clofe —	11	0	0										—	—	—		7	0	3	17	0
Barton-holds, in two parcels, —	9	3	38										—	—	—		9	0	4	10	0
Bull-Ings, in three parcels —										18	1	12	—	—	—		15	0	13	14	0
Far-field —							10	2	12				—	—	—		15	0	7	18	0
Oldbyhead Clofe —							11	0	19				—	—	—		10	0	5	11	0
The Whinny Field —							20	1	11				—	—	—		6	0	6	1	0
Long Meadow —										16	1	0	—	—	—		20	0	16	5	0
26 Lands in Thislo Common-Field —				30	2	10							—	—	—		6	0	9	3	6
Total	38	3	18	30	2	10	59	1	19	34	2	12	163	1	19				L. 85	8	4

NB. The abatement of 3 l. 8 s. 4 d. a year less than the value, is in confideration of this Tenant's being oblig'd to divide the larger Parcels of the Pafture and Meadow into fmaller ones, in order to improve them.

to his LORD.

Tenant's Name, and Lands.	Arable inclos'd.			Common Arable.			Pasture.			Meadow.			Total Number of Acres.			Yearly Value per Acre.	Yearly value of the several Parcels.		
	a	r	p	a	r	p	a	r	p	a	r	p	a	r	p	at	l.	s.	d.
Total																			

Tenant's Name, and Lands.	Arable inclos'd (a r p)	Common Arable (a r p)	Pasture (a r p)	Meadow (a r p)	Total Number of Acres (a r p)	Yearly Value per Acre. at (s. d.)	Yearly value of the several Parcels. (l. s. d.)
John Hill, for the Castle Farm.							
N° (3) { Old Rent — — 69:13:4 New Rent — — 88:0:0 } (l. s. d.)							
A *Messuage*, with Barns, Stable, Yard, &c. and a Croft adjoyning			2 1 0		—	20:0	2 5 0
Oldby Closes, in two parcels	19 0 11				—	15:0	14 6 0
Odus Field	11 1 13				—	13:0	7 6 6
Stoney Field	7 0 5				—	6:0	2 2 0
Smales Closes, in three parcels			24 0 30		—	12:0	14 9 0
Long Close			6 1 12		—	15:0	4 14 0
Long Meadow				9 0 31	—	25:0	13 7 0
Kirk-how Close			9 3 21		—	11:0	5 8 6
The Launder Flatts, in three parcels			12 1 10		—	15:0	9 4 0
Bull Meadow				11 0 0	—	20:0	11 0 0
26 Lands in Castle Common-Field		18 0 29			—	5:0	4 10 6
Total	37 1 29	18 0 29	55 0 3	20 0 31	130 3 12	L.	88 12 6

Tenant's Name, and Lands.	Arable inclos'd.			Common Arable.			Pasture.			Meadow.			Total Number of Acres.			Yearly Value per Acre.	Yearly value of the several Parcels.		
	a	r	p	a	r	p	a	r	p	a	r	p	a	r	p	at	l.	s.	d.
Total																			

Dd

Tenant's Name, and Lands.	Arable inclos'd. a r p	Common Arable. a r p	Pasture. a r p	Meadow. a r p	Total Number of Acres. a r p	Yearly Value per Acre. at s. d.	Yearly value of the several Parcels. l. s. d.
John Scot, for Eccleſhal Farm. N° (4) { Old Rent —— 80:6:8 / New Reat —— 110:0:0 }							
A Meſſuage, with Barns, Stable, Yard and Garden, and a Home-Cloſe adjoyning			3 0 0			25 : 0	3 15 0
Church Cloſe			7 3 38			15:0	6 0 0
Priors Cloſe			9 1 21			15:0	7 1 0
St. Peters Field	8 2 10					12:0	5 2 6
Nuns Cloſes, in four parcels			28 2 5			11:0	17 4 0
Snout-end Cloſe			9 0 15			10:0	4 11 6
The Park Cloſes, in two parcels			15 0 0			15:0	11 5 0
Dale Croft, in three parcels	27 0 7					9:0	12 3 0
Cow-hill Field	9 1 3					8:0	3 14 0
Lairh Cloſe			3 0 5			17:0	2 11 0
Eccleſwal Meadows, in four parcels				24 1 11		25:0	30 7 0
35 Lands in Caſtle Common-Field		29 3 9				5:0	7 9 0
Total	44 3 20	29 3 9	76 0 4	24 1 11	175 0 4		L. 111 3 0

NB. The whole is Tythe-free.

Tenant's Name, and Lands.	Arable inclos'd.			Common Arable.			Pasture.			Meadow.			Total Number of Acres.			Yearly Value per Acre.	Yearly value of the several Parcels.
	a	*r*	*p*	*a*	*r*	*p*	*a*	*r*	*p*	*a*	*r*	*p*	*a*	*r*	*p*	at	*l. s. d.*
Total																	

Tenant's Name, and Lands.	Arable inclos'd a r p	Common Arable a r p	Pasture a r p	Meadow a r p	Total Number of Acres a r p	Yearly Value per Acre. at	Yearly value of the several Parcels. l s d
Robert Ravens, for **Bagnum** Farm.							
N° (5) { Old Rent — 56:13:4 / New Rent — 65:0:0 }							
A *Messuage*, with Barns, Stable, Yard, &c. and a Garth adjoyning			1 2 37			20:0	1 15 0
The Dial Banks	7 3 9					7:0	2 13 6
The Cliff Hills	9 3 10					6:0	2 19 0
The Boor Flatts	12 1 9					11:0	6 15 0
Abraham Clofes, in two parcels			17 2 30			15:0	13 6 0
Nether Clofe			4 1 15			12:0	2 12 0
Far Clofe			10 0 0			9:0	4 10 0
Laith Clofe			18 3 11			10:0	9 8 0
Bull Ings				18 0 9		20:0	18 0 0
31 Lands in Caftle Common-Field		13 0 10				5:0	3 5 0
Total	29 3 28	13 0 10	52 2 13	18 0 9	113 2 20		L. 65 3 6

Tenant's Name, and Lands.	Arable inclos'd.			Common Arable.			Pasture.			Meadow.			Total Number of Acres.			Yearly Value *per Acre.*	Yearly value of the several Parcels.		
	a	*r*	*p*	*a*	*r*	*p*	*a*	*r*	*p*	*a*	*r*	*p*	*a*	*r*	*p*	at	*l.*	*s.*	*d.*
Total																			

E e

Tenant's Name, and Lands.	Arable inclos'd. a	r	p	Common Arable. a	r	p	Pasture. a	r	p	Meadow. a	r	p	Total Number of Acres. a	r	p	Yearly Value per Acre. at s.	d.	Yearly value of the several Parcels. l.	s.	d.
William Vaux, for Thiflo Farm.																				
Nº (6) { Old Rent ——— 80:0:0 / New Rent ——— 89:0:0 }																				
A *Messuage*, with Barns, Stable, Yard, &c. and Garth adjoyning, —							3	1	21							20:	0	3	7	6
Twin-yates, in two parcels, —	15	0	0													11:	0	8	5	0
Rye Clofe —	9	1	0													10:	0	4	13	0
Howle-Horkham Clofe —	8	3	15													9:	0	3	19	6
Eel-pye Clofe —							12	1	18							15:	0	9	5	0
Broad Clofe —							11	3	27							14:	0	8	7	0
The High Clofe —							9	2	16							17:	0	8	3	6
The Mill Butts —							8	3	13							20:	0	8	16	0
Casket Ings —										13	3	35				25:	0	17	9	0
Wood Meadow —										9	2	15				25:	0	11	18	0
20 Lands in Thiflo Common-Field, —				17	3	10										6:	0	5	5	0
Total	33	0	25	17	3	10	46	0	15	23	2	10	120	2	20			L. 89	3	6

Tenant's Name, and Lands.	Arable inclos'd.			Common Arable.			Pasture.			Meadow.			Total Number of Acres.			Yearly Value per Acre.	Yearly value of the several Parcels		
	a	r	p	a	r	p	a	r	p	a	r	p	a	r	p	at	l.	s.	d.
Total																			

Tenant's Name, and Lands.	Arable inclos'd. a	r	p	Common Arable. a	r	p	Pasture. a	r	p	Meadow. a	r	p	Total Number of Acres. a	r	p	Yearly Value per Acre. at s.	d.	Yearly value of the feveral Parcels. l.	s.	d.
David Robinfon, for Roft-hill Farm.																				
N° (7) { Old Rent —— 49:13:4 / New Rent —— 72:0:0																				
A *Meffuage*, with Barns, Stables, Yard, &c. and Garth adjoyning,							2	0	0				—	—	—	20 :	0	2	0	0
Roft-hill Clofes, in two parcels,	27	3	11										—	—	—	7 :	0	9	15	0
Calice Clofe	9	1	19										—	—	—	8 :	0	3	14	0
Nettle Dale							12	0	0				—	—	—	13 :	0	7	16	0
The Ridings, in two parcels,							21	3	39				—	—	—	12 :	0	13	14	0
Ownfow Clofe							11	3	38				—	—	—	10 :	0	6	0	0
Cliff Clofe							8	1	18				—	—	—	8 :	0	3	6	6
Cutler Ings, in two parcels,										19	2	7	—	—	—	20 :	0	19	10	6
24 Lands in the Priory Common-field,				20	1	17							—	—	—	7 :	0	7	2	0
Total	37	0	30	20	1	17	56	1	15	19	2	7	133	1	29			L. 72	18	0

to his LORD.

Tenant's Name, and Lands.	Arable inclos'd.			Common Arable.			Pasture.			Meadow.			Total Number of Acres.			Yearly Value *per* Acre.	Yearly value of the several Parcels.		
	a	r	p	a	r	p	a	r	p	a	r	p	a	r	p	at	l.	s.	d.
Total																			

Tenant's Name, and Lands.

Daniel Cole, for Dale-House Farm.

N° (8) { Old Rent ————— 40 : 13 : 4 / New Rent ————— 74 : 0 : 0 } (*l. s. d.*)

Tenant's Name, and Lands.	Arable inclos'd.			Common Arable.			Pasture.			Meadow.			Total Number of Acres.			Yearly Value per Acre. at		Yearly value of the several Parcels.		
	a	*r*	*p*	*a*	*r*	*p*	*a*	*r*	*p*	*a*	*r*	*p*	*a*	*r*	*p*	*s.*	*d.*	*l.*	*s.*	*d.*
A *Messuage*, with Barns, Stables, Yard, &c. and a Garth adjoyning							1	3	5							20	0	1	15	0
Pipers Clofes, in two parcels	17	1	15													9	0	7	15	6
Raffle-Ridge Clofe	8	0	0													8	0	3	4	0
Lay-Field	6	1	13													9	0	3	6	6
The Sweet-heads, in two parcels							3	0	0							12	0	18	0	0
Well Clofe							11	3	7							15	0	8	17	0
The Bents, in two parcels							8	2	14							13	0	5	11	6
The Welt Ings, in two parcels										2	1	0				20	0	21	0	0
27 Lands in Priory Common-Field				16	3	10										7	0	5	17	6
Total	31	2	28	16	3	10	52	0	26	21	0	0	121	2	24			L. 75	7	0

to his LORD.

Tenant's Name, and Lands.	Arable inclos'd.			Common Arable.			Pasture.			Meadow.			Total Number of Acres.			Yearly Value per Acre.	Yearly value of the several Parcels.		
	a	r	p	a	r	p	a	r	p	a	r	p	a	r	p	at	l.	s.	d.
Total																			

The Duty of a Steward

Tenant's Name, and Lands.	Arable inclos'd. a | r | p	Common Arable. a | r | p	Pasture. a | r | p	Meadow. a | r | p	Total Number of Acres. a | r | p	Yearly Value per Acre. at s. d.	Yearly value of the feveral Parcels. l. s. d.
John Cox, for Weatherhill Farm.							
Nº (9) { Old Rent — — — 38:0:0 { New Rent — — — 40:0:0							
A Meſſuage, with Barns, Stables, Yard, &c. and a Garth adjoyning	—	—	1 3 0	—	—	20 : 0	1 15 0
Cock-line Clofe — — —	5 3 17	—	—	—	—	10 : 0	2 18 6
Breary Clofe — — —	8 1 5	—	—	—	—	11 : 0	4 11 0
Barton-hold Clofe — — —	3 0 24	—	—	—	—	12 : 0	1 17 0
The Dun-Bogs Clofes, in two parcels	—	—	17 2 21	—	—	11 : 0	9 13 6
The Lay Clofes, in two parcels, —	—	—	12 0 15	—	—	10 : 0	6 1 0
The Low-Ings Clofes, in two parcels, —	—	—	—	11 3 35	—	20 : 0	12 0 0
20 Lands in Cogdale Common-Field,	—	10 1 21	—	—	—	5 : 0	2 12 0
Total	17 1 6	10 1 21	31 1 36	11 3 39	71 0 22	L.	41 8 0

NB. This Farm was advanc'd Twenty years fince; as appears by an old Rental.

Tenant's Name, and Lands.	Arable inclos'd.	Common Arable.	Pasture.	Meadow.	Total Number of Acres.	Yearly Value per Acre.	Yearly value of the several Parcels.
	a r p	a r p	a r p	a r p	a r p	at	l. s. d.

Tenant's Name, and Lands.	Arable inclos'd. a r p	Common Arable. a r p	Pasture. a r p	Meadow. a r p	Total Number of Acres. a r p	Yearly Value per Acre. at s. d.	Yearly value of the several Parcels. l. s. d.
Richard Bland, for **Blakes** Farm. N° (10) { Old Rent —— 70:0:0 { New Rent —— 74:0:0							
A *Messuage*, with Barn, Stable, Yard, &c. and Garth adjoyning,			3 1 0		—	20:0	3 5 0
The Hill Close, in two parcels, ——	8 1 33				—	8:0	3 8 0
Lakes Field —— —— ——	9 3 1				—	12:0	6 0 0
The High Field —— ——	7 0 0				—	11:0	3 17 0
The Low Field —— ——			11 3 11		—	15:0	8 17 0
Barton-Holds, in two parcels, ——			21 1 12		—	12:0	12 16 0
Cogdale Ings, in two parcels, ——				19 3 7	—	25:0	24 14 0
22 Lands in Cogdale Common-Field,		10 1 17			—	5:0	2 11 0
Total	25 1 24	10 1 17	36 1 23	19 3 7	91 3 11		L. 175 8 0

NB. This Farm also was advanc'd Twenty years since; as appears by an old Rental.

Tenant's Name, and Lands.	Arable inclos'd.			Common Arable.			Pasture.			Meadow.			Total Number of Acres.			Yearly Value per Acre.	Yearly value of the several Parcels.
	a	r	p	a	r	p	a	r	p	a	r	p	a	r	p	at	l. s. d.
Total																	

An ABSTRACT from all the foregoing Particulars.

Nº	Tenants Names, and Farms.	Arable inclos'd. a r p	Common Arable. a r p	Pasture. a r p	Meadow. a r p	Total Number of Acres. a r p	Old Rents. l. s.	New Rents agreed on or Leases. l. s. d.	Yearly value of the several Farms. l. s. d.
1	Robert Hunt, for the Priory Farm	43 2 3	21 1 39	85 2 10	19 1 32	169 3 35	80 0	105 0 0	110 17 6
2	Thomas Newton, for Blyth Farm	38 3 18	30 2 19	59 1 19	34 2 12	163 1 19	68	82 0 0	85 8 4
3	John Hill, for the Castle Farm	37 1 29	18 0 29	55 0 3	20 0 31	130 3 12	69 13 4	88 0 0	88 12 6
4	John Scot, for Eckelwal Farm	44 3 20	29 3 9	76 0 4	24 1 11	175 0 4	80 0 8	110 0 0	111 3 0
5	Robert Ravens, for Bagmor Farm	29 3 28	13 0 10	52 2 13	18 0 9	113 3 20	56 13 4	65 0 0	65 3 6
6	William Vaux, for Thilo Farm	33 0 25	17 3 19	46 0 15	23 2 10	120 2 20	80 0 0	89 0 0	89 8 6
7	David Robinson, for Roft-hill Farm	37 0 30	20 1 17	56 1 15	19 2 7	133 1 29	40 13 4	72 0 0	72 18 0
8	Daniel Cole, for Dale-house Farm	31 2 28	16 3 10	52 0 26	21 0 0	121 2 24	40 13 4	74 0 0	75 7 0
9	John Cox, for Weather-hill Farm,	17 1 6	10 1 21	31 1 36	11 3 39	71 0 22	38 0 0	40 0 0	41 8 0
10	Richard Bland, for Blakes Farm	25 1 24	10 1 17	36 1 23	19 3 7	91 3 31	70 0 0	74 0 0	75 8 0
	Total Amount of this Manor —	339 1 11	188 3 3	550 0 4	212 1 38	1291 2 16	624 6 8	799 0 0	815 14 4

```
                                   l.   s.  d.
NB. { New Rents agreed on —799 : 0 : 0
      Old Rents —————624 : 6 : 8
Total Improvement in this Manor,—174 : 13 : 4
```

to his LORD.

An ABSTRACT *from all the* foregoing *Particulars.*

Tenants Names, and Farms.	Arable inclos'd.			Common Arable.			Pasture.			Meadow.			Total Number of Acres.			Old Rents.			New Rents agreed on for Leases.			Yearly value of the several Farms.		
	a	r	p	a	r	p	a	r	p	a	r	p	a	r	p	l.	s.	d.	l.	s.	d.	l.	s.	d.
Total Amount of this Manor																								

An

An Abſtract of

General Covenants

To be obſerv'd by

All the 'foreſaid Tenants in the aforeſaid Manor of *K——*, which I left with the Steward of the Court, in order to be inſerted in all the aforemention'd Tenants Leaſes.

NB. *Theſe* Covenants *will prove of General Uſe to moſt Eſtates.*

Covenant I.

THAT **all** the Tenants in the ſaid *Manor* ſhall be oblig'd not to *pare* and *burn* any part or parcel of the Lands in their Farms; the practiſing of this having been found by long Experience to be very Prejudicial to Lands, becauſe it draws out moſt of the *Nitrous Particles* fit for vegetation. Therefore any one of the Tenants, that ſhall be Guilty of this Offence, ſhall pay (over and above his yearly Rent) the Sum of Twenty pounds for every Acre pared and burnt as aforeſaid.

Cove-

✿✿✿✿✿✿✿✿✿✿✿✿✿✿✿✿✿✿✿ ✿✿✿✿✿✿✿✿✿✿✿✿✿✿✿✿✿✿

Covenant II.

THAT all the said Tenants shall be oblig'd not to sow any *Rape*, *Hemp*, *Flax*, *Woad*, *Weld*, *Madder*, &c. on any part or parcel of their Lands; nor to plant any *Potatoes*, or *Hops*, (except in small quantities for their own use) on the Penalty of paying, *over* and *above* their *yearly* Rent, the Sum of Ten pounds for every Acre of Land on which they shall *sow* or *plant* any of the abovemention'd Vegetables, without further Covenants, in order to pay a valuable consideration for the same, and also to lay down the Lands for Pasture in a good ✳ condition.

✳ As these Vegetables breed no Manure, so great Care (by a strict Covenant) should be taken that the Lands are laid down in a good condition, *i. e.* by re-enriching them with Twenty Load of Dung (over and above what the Farm produces) or a Hundred Bushels of Lime, upon an Acre. If such a Covenant is not duly observ'd, 'twill be the same prejudice to the Lands, as selling the Hay and Straw off the Premises.

Cove=

Covenant III.

THAT all the said Tenants shall be oblig'd not to plow up, nor convert into Tillage, any part or parcels of any Inclosure, as is specified in the Particulars under the proper Columns of Pasture and Meadow, on Penalty of paying Ten pound for every Acre so plow'd, to be paid *over* and *above* their yearly Rent. And if any part of the said Inclosures shall happen to grow over with *Moss*, *Prie*, or other *Coarse Grass*, then the said Tenants (Leave being first granted) may plow up the same, or convert it into Tillage, in order to improve the same, for the space of Three years only : Provided always that the said Tenants shall, the Spring following, be oblig'd to lay down the said Lands with *Clover*, *Rey-grass*, or other proper *Grass-Seeds*, as shall be thought most agreeable to the nature of the Land. But before the said Tenants begin to plow up the said Pastures or Meadows, *timely* notice before-hand shall be given to the proper *Agent* or *Steward* appointed by the Lord of the Manor, that they may be Judges whether the said Pastures or Meadows will not suffer damage by a *moderate* plowing. And also the said Tenants (before they begin to plow the aforesaid Pasture and Meadow) shall consent to pay a *valuable* consideration (according to the Goodness of the Land) to be paid *over* and *above* their yearly Rent, for the advantage of plowing up fresh Pasture or Meadow-ground, to be agreed on first by the Steward and Tenant.

Cove=

Covenant IV.

THAT all the said Tenants shall be oblig'd not to cut down any Timber-trees, Saplins, Pollards, or Underwoods on any part of their Farms, on Penalty of paying *over* and *above* their yearly Rent ten times the value of the same, except only what is necessary for Repairs of their Houses ; and this to be assign'd them by the proper Agent or Steward.

Covenant V.

THAT all the said Tenants shall be oblig'd to observe and practise the following due Course of Husbandry in the inclos'd Lands, *viz.* the *first* year after the fallow, to sow Wheat, Rye, or Barley ; the *second*, to sow Beans or Pease, or rather Both **Under=Furrow** ; the *third*, to sow Barley or Oates ; and the *fourth* year, to let the Land lie for Fallow ; which Covenant is calculated for the good both of the Farms and the Farmer : And, that the

I i

said

said Tenants fhall be oblig'd to lay upon their Pafture and Meadow-ground at leaft one half of the Dung which their Farms produce, and the other half upon the Tillage-Land.   And, to reftore the Riches of the Tillage, each Tenant, every year, fhall be oblig'd to lay Forty Bufhels of Lime upon every Acre off *their* Land lying fallow, (a) which, according to the 'foregoing Courfe of Husbandry, muft be a fourth part of what is allotted them for Tillage, fpecified under the proper Columns of *Arable Inclos'd* and *Common Arable*.   And alfo, that each Tenant fhall be oblig'd, every year, to feed or Summer-pafture about one fourth part of their Meadows; fo that the whole quantity of Meadowing, may be Summer-eaten once in four years : The due obferving of this, will eftablifh that known *Maxim* amongft the moft experienc'd Farmers, that *mowing of Lands too often and too long*, is as great a Prejudice to them as *too often and too long plowing them is to Tillage*, except plenty of *fuperinduЄtions* of Dungs, *&c.* can be had with eafe. Any one of the Tenants not performing every part of this Fifth Covenant, fhall be oblig'd to pay, *over* and *above* his yearly Rent, the Sum of Twenty pounds.

(a) Where 'tis the Cuftom for new Tenants to enter at *Michaelmas*, then the old Tenant fhou'd be oblig'd to leave a fourth part of his Tillage well fallow'd (by giving the fame four tills or plowings) to the new Tenant, he paying a reafonable price for the fame, according to cuftom.

Covenant VI.

THAT all the said Tenants shall be oblig'd to spend all the Hay and Straw upon the Premises; and at the end of their Leases or term of years, to leave all, both Dung and Straw, to the succeeding Tenant, without any consideration for the same. And the better to perform this Article, tho' their Leases expire at *Lady-day,* yet nevertheless the said Tenants (if they leave their Farms) may have liberty till *May-day* following to make use of the Barns to thrash out their Corn, and also to make use of the Fold-yard. The said Tenants not performing every part of this Article, shall be oblig'd to pay, *over* and *above* their yearly Rent, the Sum of Twenty pounds.

Cove=

Covenant VII.

THat **all** the said Tenants shall be oblig'd to cleanse
and scowre up their Ditches in a Husbandlike manner, in order to carry off the Water in such manner as
(if possible) not to let the Water *settle* or *stagnate* any where
in the *lower* part of the Grounds, on Penalty of paying Ten
pounds for such neglect.

Covenant VIII.

THat **all** the said Tenants shall be oblig'd, at their
own proper Cost and Charge, to keep up their
Messuages or Dwelling-Houses in good and tenantable repair, and to leave the same to the succeeding Tenant without any consideration for the same, they being allow'd
rough Timber, and Stone from the Quarries, such as the
Estate produces.

Cove=

Covenant IX.

THAT all the said Tenants shall be oblig'd to yoke and ring their Hogs, to prevent damage to the Fences, and rooting up the Pasture-Grounds, on the Penalty of paying Ten shillings for each Hog suffer'd to be unrung or unyoked.

Covenant X.

THAT all the said Tenants shall be oblig'd to sow their Winter Corn (if possible) rather before than after *Michaelmas* (which by Experience is found to be most suitable to the Northern parts.) In like manner the Summer Corn (if possible) to be sown *before Lady-day*, in order to *forward* the Harvest. Also the said Tenants shall be oblig'd to *Hayn* (*i.e.* clear their Meadows of the Cattle) at *Lady-day*, on the Penalty of paying Ten pounds for this and the foregoing Neglect.

K k

Cove=

Covenant XI.

THAT all the said Tenants shall be oblig'd not to let out any part of their Farms to any *Under-Tenant*, the doing of which having been found to be very *prejudicial* to most Estates. The said Tenants therefore shall pay *over* and *above* their yearly Rents, the Sum of Twenty pounds for every part or parcel so let out as abovemention'd.

Covenant XII.

THAT all the said Tenants shall be oblig'd to cut and plash their Hedges in a Husband-like manner, at about twelve years growth from the time of their first planting; and also to nurse up the same by weeding. The neglect of doing these has been the ruin of most Fences in the North of *England*; therefore any Tenant that neglects the doing of this *great* piece of service to *Himself*, as well as the *Lord of the Manor*, shall pay, *over* and *above* his yearly Rent, the Sum of Twenty pounds.

Cove=

Covenant XIII.

THAT all the said Tenants shall be oblig'd not to stock any part of their Farm with Rabbits, the doing of this having been found by long Experience to be very prejudicial to Estates, especially upon a dry sandy Soil; therefore any one of the Tenants, that shall be guilty of this, shall pay, *over* and *above* his yearly Rent, the Sum of Two hundred pounds for such offence.

Covenant XIV.

THAT all the said Tenants shall be oblig'd not to gather the Cow-dung together on heaps, first to dry it, and then to burn it instead of Wood and Coal; the doing of this also having been found to be very prejudicial to Estates, because it robs the Land of one of the best sorts of Manures: Therefore any one of the Tenants that shall be guilty of this, shall pay, *over* and *above* his yearly Rent, the Sum of Ten pounds for such offence.

Cove-

Covenant XV.

THAT **all** the said Tenants shall be oblig'd to pay the *Mole-catcher*, after the rate of 12 *d.* a dozen for what he destroys; and, that *each Tenant* do pay in proportion to the bigness of his Farm, which is to be adjusted by the Steward. If any one of the Tenants refuses to pay his Dividend, then it shall be in the power of the Steward to charge it to his yearly Rent.

Covenant XVI.

THAT **all** the said Tenants shall be oblig'd (at their own proper cost and charge) to keep the Bye-roads leading through their Grounds in good and sufficient repair, by laying and keeping them *dry*; and afterwards to make them lie *round* and *high* in the middle; and, when the Earth is well settled at Midsummer, to lay all the Gravel-stones that can be got upon it: This will be a means to prevent Travellers from poaching on each side, to the no small detriment of a Farm. Any one of the Tenants not performing this Article, shall pay, *over* and *above* his yearly Rent, the Sum of Ten pounds for such Neglect.

Cove=

Covenant XVII.

THAT all the said Tenants shall be oblig'd not to keep any Greyhounds, Guns, &c. nor to set any Snares, Ginns, &c. so as to destroy the Lord's Game in any sort; nor to trace any Hares in the Snow. Any one of the Tanants that is guilty of this Offence shall pay, *over* and *above* his yearly Rent, the Sum of Five pounds.

Covenant XVIII.

THAT all the said Tenants shall be oblig'd not to commit waste in any sort upon any part of their Farms, especially by erecting Brick-kilns, and by digging Clay in order to make Bricks for sale, without further Covenants, in order to pay a valuable consideration for the same. Any one of the Tenants, not duly performing this Covenant, shall pay, *over* and *above* his yearly Rent, the Sum of Five hundred pounds.

L l

Cove=

Covenant XIX.

THAT all the said Tenants shall be oblig'd (whenever the Lord of the Manor or his Steward demands it) to send their Teams to lead home the Hay and Corn which comes off the Demesne Lands only, kept in hand for the Lord's use ; and also to lead home Stone or Timber whenever he has occasion for Building or Repairs. Any one of the Tenants not performing this Covenant, shall pay, *over* and *above* his yearly Rent, the Sum of Five pounds for such Neglect.

Covenant XX.

AS the Lord of the Manor has been at an extraordinary Charge in covering the Farm-house and Out-houses with Slate and Tile, instead of thatching them with *Straw*; so all the said Tenants shall be oblig'd, at their own cost and charge for the future, to keep them up in the like repair ; not only as a better security against the Accidents
dents

dents and Misfortunes by Fire, but that it robbs the Land of great quantities of Manure that the said thatching with Straw would produce. Any one of the Tenants not duly performing this Covenant, shall pay, *over* and *above* his yearly Rent, the Sum of Twenty pounds for such Neglect.

Covenant XXI.

THAT **all** the said Tenants in the said Manor shall be oblig'd to pay the Church, Poor, and Constable's Assessments, and *all* other Taxes and Assessments whatsoever, except the Land-Tax.

Covenant XXII.

THAT **all** the said Tenants shall be oblig'd every *Christmas*, or some other time of the Year as shall be adjudg'd most acceptable, to send a Present to his Lord of two fat Capons, or two fat Turkeys, or two fat Geese, or
any

any other Fowl, or Fish of the like value ; on Penalty of paying Ten shillings *over* and *above* their yearly Rent for such Neglect.

NB. It may be objected by *many*, that several of these Covenants might have been omitted, because they are *presentable* at the Court-Baron ; but let such consider how *little* these matters of *consequence* have been regarded of late years at these Courts, because too many Stewards are indolent, and the Tenants *combine* together, and will not present one another : Therefore the most effectual remedy to have Covenants strictly observ'd, is to have recourse to Common Law.

The aforegoing Articles are only heads of Covenants ; and tho' the reasons of them are there assign'd, yet the putting them in proper forms of Law, and wording them, is left to the discretion of the Lawyer.

Note also, 'Twou'd be very proper to have a Plan annex'd to each Lease, with the Particulars in the manner 'foregoing ; and likewise an 𝕬𝖇𝖘𝖙𝖗𝖆𝖈𝖙 of the Covenants joyn'd with the said Particulars, that they may be more readily look'd into upon occasion.

AND for the greater satisfaction of every Nobleman and Gentleman, 'tis adviseable to have three parts of the Leases executed, each by the Leasor and Leasee, one to be kept by the Lord of the Manor, another by the Steward, and the third by the Tenant. This will most certainly prevent many wilful Mistakes, which otherwise in an ill-dispos'd Steward may impose upon the Lord of the Manor by 𝕱𝖔𝖗𝖌𝖊𝖗𝖞, &c.

A

A
Plain and Easy Method

To be practis'd by every

STEWARD

IN

Keeping his *Accompts* in such a manner
as to be readily examin'd.

First, By Entering down ALL the *Articles* of the several
Kinds for Money Receiv'd distinctly by themselves, with
the Sum Total of each Kind.

Secondly, By Entering down ALL the Articles of the
several Kinds of Disbursements distinctly by themselves,
with the Sum Total of each Kind.

Thirdly, and lastly, By drawing up an Abstract, or an
Accompt-Current by way of Debtor and Creditor, from
ALL the 'foremention'd Particulars, in order to shew
the exact Balance.

M m   *NB.*

NB. I publiſh theſe Accompts not only for the Uſe of ſuch Stewards who are *better* qualified in Country Buſineſs than in Accompts, but alſo to ſhew an Example of what Articles ſhou'd be charg'd as Receiv'd for the Lord's Uſe, which was formerly thought to be a Steward's Perquiſite.

It may be very proper the Steward ſhou'd keep a Caſh-book and Journal, according to the Common Method, for his own private Uſe and Satisfaction; but ſome ſuch following Methods ſhould always be deliver'd to his Lord, in order to their more eaſy Examination by him.

𝔄𝔫

An Account

Of the *several Sums of Money Received from the four several Manors of* G, H, I, K, *in the* County *of* H, *by* A. B. *Steward to His Grace the Duke of* K.

For One whole Year,

From *Lady-day* 1725 to *Lady-day* 1726.

A Rental for the Manor of *G.* in the County of *H.* Receiv'd by *A. B.* Steward to His Grace the Duke of *K.* Being One whole Year's Rent from *Lady-day* 1725 to *Lady-day* 1726.	Yearly Rents.		
Nº	*l.*	*s.*	*d.*
1 *Roger Cooper,* for the 𝕸𝖆𝖓𝖔𝖗 𝖔𝖋 𝕶. Farm and Demeſnes	210	0	0
2 *William Rogers,* for the 𝖂𝖊𝖑𝖑-𝖍𝖔𝖚𝖘𝖊 Farm	95	10	0
3 *George Atkinſon,* for 𝕽𝖎𝖉𝖑𝖊𝖞's Farm	82	10	0
4 *Robert Atkinſon,* for 𝕽𝖔𝖇𝖔𝖙𝖙𝖔𝖒's Farm	65	0	0
5 *Lawrence Davidſon,* for 𝕮𝖗𝖔𝖜𝖑𝖊𝖞's Farm	48	10	0
6 *Abraham Jackſon,* for 𝕭𝖗𝖔𝖆𝖉 Farm	37	0	0
7 *Abraham Cooling,* for the 𝕮𝖔𝖑𝖉-𝕭𝖆𝖙𝖍 Farm	36	10	0
8 *Jonathan Caverly,* for 𝕭𝖑𝖆𝖈𝖐𝖘𝖒𝖎𝖙𝖍's Farm	31	0	0
9 *Gabriel Badcock,* for the 𝕲𝖎𝖑𝖑 Farm	28	10	0
10 *John Reynolds,* for the 𝕭𝖚𝖘𝖐𝖞 Farm	20	15	0
11 *David Bigg,* for the 𝕻𝖆𝖗𝖐-𝖕𝖔𝖓𝖉 Farm	20	10	0
12 *Nathaniel Bigg,* for 𝕯𝖔𝖛𝖊𝖍𝖔𝖚𝖘𝖊 Farm	17	15	0
13 *Mavy Goodchild,* for her Houſe in *Crowley,* and Lake's Lands	8	5	0
14 *Tho. North,* for a Houſe and Cloſe in *Crowley,*	3	10	0
15 *Geo. Caverly,* for a Houſe and Cloſe in *Crowley*	2	5	0
16 *Tho. Caverly,* for a Houſe and Cloſe in *Crowley*	2	0	0
17 *Jane Goodchild,* for a Houſe and Cloſe in *Crowley,*	1	15	0
18 *Mary Cooper,* for a Houſe and Cloſe in *Crowley*	1	10	0
19 *John Davidſon,* for a Houſe and Cloſe in *Crowley,*	1	5	0
20 *John Blackbourn,* for a Houſe and Cloſe in *Crowley,*	1	5	0
21 *David Robinſon,* for a Houſe and Cloſe in *Crowley,*	1	0	0
Receiv'd of the ſeveral *Copyholders of Inheritance* their Quit-Rents, as appears yearly in the Copy of Court-roll for this Manor	18	17	5
Total Amount of this Manor	735	2	5

A

A Rental for the Manor of *H.* in the County of of *H.* receiv'd by *A. B.* Steward to His Grace the Duke of *K.* Being One whole Year's Rent from *Lady-day* 1725 to *Lady-day* 1726.	Yearly Rents.		
N°	*l.*	*s.*	*d*
1	*John Hill*, for the 𝕳all Farm and Demesnes — —	170	0	0
2	*Roger Hill*, for 𝕭ernard's Farm — — — — —	65	10	0
3	*John Manners*, for the 𝕽idge=house Farm — —	62	0	0
4	*William Stonehouse*, for 𝕻aradise Farm — — —	60	10	0
5	*Edward Barlow*, for the ff enn Farm — — — —	47	0	0
6	*Benjamin Butler*, for the 𝕿albot=𝕵nn Farm — —	43	10	0
7	*Mary Johnson*, for the 𝖂ilderness Farm — — —	38	0	0
8	*Mary Scott*, for ff letcher's Farm — — — — —	24	10	0
9	*Elizabeth Mary-gold*, for the 𝕯ale Farm — — —	20	15	0
10	*Christopher Thompson*, for 𝕺ldby's Farm — — —	20	0	0
11	*Margery Rogers*, for 𝕽abie's Farm — — — —	18	0	0
12	*Thomas Masterman*, for 𝕲regory's Farm — — —	16	10	0
13	*Thomas Ball*, for 𝕹utt's Farm — — — — —	15	15	0
14	*William Bernard*, for 𝕭lake's Farm — — — —	12	0	0
15	*John Gill*, for the 𝕷ow Farm — — — — —	11	0	0
16	*Jane Hansel*, for *Tanner's* Lands — — — — —	9	5	0
17	*Roger Mason*, for the Road-lands — — — — —	9	0	0
18	*Margery Snell*, for a House and Close in *Denton* —	2	10	0
Total Amount of this Manor —	645	15	0

N n

A Ren-

A Rental for the Manor of *I.* in the County of *H.* Receiv'd by *A. B.* Steward to His Grace the Duke of *K.* Being One whole Year's Rent from *Lady-day* 1725 to *Lady-day* 1726.	Yearly Rents.		
N°	*l.*	*s.*	*d.*
1 *James Wilson*, for **Rousby** Farm — — — — — —	130	0	0
2 *Roger Vaux*, for **Skelton**'s Farm — — — — —	100	0	0
3 *John Turner*, for **Manwaring**'s Farm — — —	100	0	0
4 *William Moss*, for **Bog-house** Farm — — — —	85	0	0
5 *Thomas Mason*, for **Dove-house** Farm — — —	82	0	0
6 *Abraham Johnson*, for the **Hall** Farm — — —	80	0	0
7 *John Forster*, for the **Fenn** Farm — — — —	76	0	0
8 *James Fysh*, for **Wath** Farm — — — — —	75	0	0
9 *John Fysh*, for **Ashome** Farm — — — — —	73	0	0
10 *Edward Trotter*, for **Lake**'s Farm — — — —	71	0	0
11 *Edward Taylor*, for **Gefferson**'s Farm — — —	70	10	0
12 *William Williams*, for **Coverdale** Farm — — —	67	0	0
13 *John Younger*, for **Laith** Farm — — — —	66	0	0
14 *William Lawrence*, for **Grimsby** Farm — — —	62	10	0
15 *Thomas Keld*, for the **Cap-house** Farm — — —	60	10	0
16 *John Thompson*, for **Angel** Farm — — — —	52	0	0
17 *James Badcock*, for **Bingley**'s Farm — — —	41	10	0
18 *Robert Jennens*, for the **Dale** Farm — — — —	32	0	0
19 *James Noakes*, for **Fogg** Farm — — — — —	21	10	0
Total of this Manor —	1345	10	0

A

A Rental for the Manor of *K*. in the County of *H*. receiv'd by *A. B.* Steward to His Grace the Duke of *K*. Being One whole Years Rent from *Lady-day* 1725 to *Lady-day* 1726.	Yearly Rents.		
N°	*l.*	*s.*	*d.*
1　*Robert Hunt*, for the 𝕻𝖗𝖎𝖔𝖗𝖞 Farm — — — — —	105	0	0
2　*Thomas Newton*, for 𝕭𝖑𝖞𝖙𝖍's Farm — — — —	82	0	0
3　*John Hill*, for the 𝕮𝖆𝖘𝖙𝖑𝖊 Farm — — — — —	88	0	0
4　*John Scot*, for 𝕰𝖈𝖈𝖑𝖊𝖘𝖜𝖆𝖑 Farm — — — — —	110	0	0
5　*Robert Ravens*, for 𝕭𝖆𝖌-𝕸𝖔𝖔𝖗 Farm — — — —	65	0	0
6　*William Vaux*, for 𝕮𝖍𝖎𝖘𝖑𝖔 Farm — — — —	89	0	0
7　*David Robinson*, for 𝕽𝖔𝖘𝖙-𝖍𝖎𝖑𝖑 Farm — — — —	72	0	0
8　*Daniel Cole*, for 𝕯𝖆𝖑𝖊-𝕳𝖔𝖚𝖘𝖊 Farm — — — —	74	0	0
9　*John Cox*, for 𝖂𝖊𝖆𝖙𝖍𝖊𝖗-𝖍𝖎𝖑𝖑 Farm — — — —	40	0	0
10　*Richard Bland*, for 𝕭𝖑𝖆𝖐𝖊's Farm — — — —	74	0	0
Total of this Manor ——	799	0	0

An 𝕬𝖇𝖘𝖙𝖗𝖆𝖈𝖙 of the Rentals from these 4 Manors, *viz.*			
1. The Manor of G. — — — — —	735	2	5
2. The Manor of H. — — — —	645	15	0
3. The Manor of I. — — — —	1345	10	0
4. The Manor of K. — — — —	799	0	0
Total Amount of the certain Rents from these 4 Manors ——	3525	7	5

An

An Account of Casual Profits of Courts by Fines, Hariots, and Surrenders, &c. from the several *Copyholders of Inheritance* within the Manor of *G.* in the County of *H.*

(At a Court-Baron held the 27th of *March*, 1725.)

	l.	*s.*	*d*
R Eceiv'd of *John Todd*, a Composition for Five Hariots, instead of his Five best Beasts or Goods, due to the Lord of the Manor at the Death of his Father *John Todd*,— — — — — — —	56	0	0
R Eceiv'd of the aforesaid *John Todd*, a Fine for his being admitted Tenant to his Father's Estate Mr. *Thomas Todd.* The Fine formerly accepted by the Lord of the Manor for this Estate used to be but 80 Pounds; but, in consideration that the value of Money is decreas'd very much of late years, the said *John Todd* agrees to pay — — — — — — —	110	0	0
R Eceiv'd of *Jonathan Cooper* a Composition for a Hariot, instead of his best Beast or Goods, due (as aforesaid) at the Death of his Father *Jonathan Cooper*, — — — — — — —	10	0	0
R Eceiv'd of the said *Jonathan Cooper*, a Fine for his being admitted Tenant to his Father's Estate aforesaid. The Fine formerly used to be but 15 Pounds; but, for the reason aforemention'd, the said *Jonathan Cooper* agrees to pay — — — —	20	0	0
R Eceiv'd of *Robert Hunt*, for an estray Gelding sold to him, which was due to the Lord of the Manor, the said *Robert Hunt* being at *all* Charges of keeping a Year and a Day, and also for crying at the several Market-Towns, — — — — — — —	7	8	3
Continued———	203	8	3

Profits

Profits of Courts continued.

(At a Court-Baron held the 9th of *October*, 1725.)

	l.	*s.*	*d*
Brought over — — — — — — — — — — — — — — — —	203	8	3
REceiv'd of *Tho. Giles* a Fine on account of a Surrender made to him of an Eftate of Mr. *Tho. Hart.* The Fine formerly accepted by the Lord of the Manor ufed to be but 60 pounds, but on the Confideration aforemention'd the faid *Tho. Giles* agrees to pay—	82	0	0
REceiv'd of the aforefaid *Tho. Giles* a Fine for his being admitted Tenant to the aforefaid *Thomas Hart*'s Eftate. The Fine formerly accepted by the Lord of the Manor for an admittance to the aforefaid Eftate ufed to be but 15 Pounds; but, for the reafon aforemention'd, the faid *Thomas Giles* agrees to pay	20	0	0
REceiv'd of *Robert Williams* a Fine on account of a Surrender of an Eftate made to him by *William Rachel.* The Fine formerly accepted by the Lord of the Manor, for the aforefaid Eftate, ufed to be but 30 pounds, but for the reafon aforemention'd the faid *Robert Williams* agrees to pay — — — — —	40	0	0
REceiv'd of the aforefaid *Robert Williams* a Fine for his being admitted Tenant to the aforefaid *William Rachel*'s Eftate. The Fine formerly for admittance to this Eftate ufed to be but 15 Pounds; but, for the reafon aforemention'd the faid *Robert Williams* agrees to pay— — — — — — — —	20	0	0
Total Amount of this Manor —	365	8	3

An Account of Cafual Profits receiv'd *over* and *above* the Yearly Rents from the feveral Tenants following, by their entering into *New Covenants* for plowing up *Frefh* Pafture-grounds in order to fow *Woad*, *Weld*, and plant *Madder* for the Dyers ufe, for three Years only, and then to lay down the faid Pafture for *Grafs* the fourth Year, by fowing the natural *Hay-feeds*, or *Rye-grafs* and *Clover* together. And, to reftore the Riches that the 'forefaid *Woad*, *Weld*, &c. may have taken from the faid Pafture, the faid Tenants alfo are oblig'd by this *New Covenant* to lay on 100 bufhels of Lime, or 20 loads of Dung, upon every Acre, at the time of laying down the faid Grounds.

	l.	*s.*	*d.*
Receiv'd of *Robert Hunt*, Tenant for the 𝔓𝔯𝔦𝔬𝔯𝔶 Farm in the Manor of *K*. for liberty of plowing up two parcels of Pafture-grounds in his Farm, call'd the *Priory Clofes*, containing acres R. P. 25 : 1 : 5 for 3 years only, for fowing *Woad* thereon, at the rate of 6 *l.* 10 *s.* per Acre for the faid 3 years, — — —	163	7	6
Receiv'd of *John Scot* Tenant for 𝔈𝔠𝔠𝔩𝔢𝔰𝔴𝔞𝔩 Farm, in the aforefaid Manor, for the like liberty of plowing up four parcels of Pafture-grounds call'd *The Nuns Clofes*, containing acres R. P. 28 : 2 : 5. for 3 years only, for fowing *Weld* thereon, at the rate of 5 *l.* 10 *s.* per Acre, for the faid 3 years — — — —	156	15	0
Receiv'd of *Daniel Cole*, Tenant for 𝔇𝔞𝔩𝔢-𝔥𝔬𝔲𝔰𝔢 Farm, in the aforefaid Manor, for the like liberty of plowing up two parcels of Pafture-ground in his Farm call'd *The Sweet-heads*, containing 30 Acres, for 3 years only, for planting *Madder* thereon, at the rate of 5 *l.* 15 *s.* per Acre for the faid 3 years — — —	172	10	0
Total of cafual Profits for plowing up frefh Pafture —	492	12	6

NB. The 'forementimn'd Articles are not always by Stewards brought to Accompt, becaufe they look upon them as Perquifites to themfelves: Which is one way that *Unjuft* Stewards take to acquire large Eftates. If Tenants break up Frefh Pafture for fowing common Grain for Three Years, the like Covenants ought to be obferv'd, and the Steward fhould make the beft Bargain he can with them: And if the Pafture is good, it may be worth about Five pounds an Acre for Three Years *over* and *above* their yearly Rent; and this the *Steward* fhould bring to Accompt. In moft Manors where there are large Commons and Waftes, the Waftes are much fubject to grow over with *Fern*, which if mow'd down and burnt in a dry feafon, the Afhes turn to a good account for the Soap-boilers ufe. This ought alfo to be brought to Accompt, with *every* thing elfe that the Eftate produceth.

An Account of the Sale of the Underwood in the Wood call'd 𝔓𝔯𝔦𝔬𝔯's 𝔚𝔬𝔬𝔡, in the Manor of *K.* in the County of *H.* containing in the whole 22 Acres, the Underwood of which being 35 Years growth.

[The Sale-day *November* 28th, 1724.]

N° of Acres.		*l.*	*s.*	*d.*
1	Sold to *Robert Hunt* — for —	14	0	0
2	Sold to *Ditto* — for —	15	10	0
3	Sold to *Thomas Newton* — for —	11	10	0
4	Sold to *Ditto* — for —	16	0	0
5	Sold to *ditto* — for —	16	10	0
6	Sold to *John Hill* — for —	10	15	0
7	Sold to *ditto* — for —	13	15	0
8	Sold to *John Scott* — for —	17	0	0
9	Sold to *Robert Ravens* — for —	18	0	0
10	Sold to *ditto* — for —	16	15	0
11	Sold to *ditto* — for —	15	15	0
12	Sold to *William Vaux* — for —	13	10	0
13	Sold to *David Robinson* — for —	11	15	0
14	Sold to *ditto* — for —	12	0	0
15	Sold to *Daniel Cole* — for —	12	0	0
16	Sold to *John Cox* — for —	12	0	0
17	Sold to *Richard Johnson* — for —	13	15	0
18	Sold to *Edward Jackson* — for —	19	10	0
19	Sold to *James Wilson* — for —	20	0	0
20	Sold to *ditto* — for —	20	10	0
21	Sold to *Mary Knowles* — for —	20	10	0
22	Sold to *ditto* — for —	18	15	0
	Total for the Sale of this Underwood —	339	15	0

NB. 'Tis the Custom in the North of *England* to sell the Underwood by the Statute-Acre, Bark and all standing, and the Person that buys it to be at all charges of felling, &c.

An

An Account of the **Bodies** of the feveral Timber-Trees fold out of the aforefaid **Prior's Wood**, containing in the whole 274 Timber-Trees.

[The Sale-day being the 30th of *November*, 1724.]

N° of Trees	Perfons Names fold to.	N° of folid Feet.	Value *per* Foot.	Value of the feveral parcels of Timb. trees		
			s. d.	*l.*	*s.*	*d*
13	fold to *John Cotterel*, containing	489	at 1 : 0 *per* foot	24	9	0
29	fold to *Will. Rogers*, containing	1456	at 1 : 2 *per* foot	84	18	8
32	fold to *James Wells*, containing	1920	at 1 : 6 *per* foot	145	10	0
24	fold to *Thomas Cox*, containing-	969	at 1 : 0 *per* foot	48	9	0
17	fold to *Thomas Law*, containing	1029	at 1 : 4 *per* foot	63	12	0
18	fold to *Roger Leng*, containing--	720	at 1 : 2 *per* foot	42	0	0
39	fold to *Will. Adams*, containing-	1574	at 1 : 3 *per* foot	98	7	6
43	fold to *Edw. Johnfon*, containing	2150	at 1 : 6 *per* foot	161	5	0
28	fold to *Ed. Norwood*, containing	1673	at 1 : 5 *per* foot	118	0	0
31	fold to *John Rogers*, containing-	1865	at 1 : 6 *per* foot	139	17	6
274	Total. Total-	13845	Total *l.*	926	8	8

NB. The aformention'd Perfons that bought this Timber were at *all* Charges of felling them, and grubbing the Rcots out of the Ground, which was given for part of the Charge of doing it.

An

An Account of the 𝕳𝖊𝖆𝖉𝖘 of the 'foregoing Timber-Trees
sold to the several Persons following, for Faggoting only :
Most of the said Timber-Trees being tall and strait, the
Heads were not of great value.

N° of the Heads of Trees	(The Sale-Day being *December* the 1st, 1724.)	*l.*	*s.*	*d*
		s. d.			
43	Sold to *Dorothy Johnson* — — at 5 : 6 each — —	11	16	6
32	Sold to *John Ridley* — — — —at 7 : 6 each — —	12	0	0
28	Sold to *Richard Alleley* — — —at 8 : 0 each — —	10	4	0
29	Sold to *Robert Holmes* — — —at 7 : 6 each — —	10	17	0
31	Sold to *Mary Rogers* — — — at 10 : 0 each— — —	15	10	0
39	Sold to *Jane Hooper* — — —— at 11 : 0 each — —	21	9	0
13	Sold to *Elizabeth Market* — —at 12 : 6 each — —	8	2	6
24	Sold to *Thomas Cox* — — — —at 13 : 0 each — —	15	12	0
18	Sold to *Margery Goodchild* — at 11 : 0 each — —	9	18	0
17	Sold to *John Robinson* — — —at 9 : 0 each — —	7	13	0
274	Total for the Heads sold —	123	2	0

NB. The Bark is excepted out of the Sale of the Heads of the said Trees, as well as
the Bodies.

An Account of the Sale of the **Bark** from the 'forefaid Timber-Trees and Heads, to the feveral Perfons following, by the yard, the faid Bark being placed a yard wide at the bottom, and a yard high, meeting in a point at top in the form of a triangular Prifm, the better to caft off the wet.

(The Sale-Day being the 24th of *April*, 1725.)

N° of yards.		*l.*	*s.*	*d.*
2970	yards fold to *Abraham Wilks*, at 13 *d. per* yard —	160	17	6
604	yards fold to *Daniel Roper*, at 13 *d. per* yard — —	32	14	2
1500	yards fold to *Thomas Fairchild*, at 13 *d. per* pard —	81	5	0
1370	yards fold to *John Whimp*, at 13 *d. per* yard — — —	74	4	2
	(NB. Thefe Perfons were at all Charges of ftripping, &c.)			
6444	Total	349	0	10

An **Abftract** of the Sale of the Underwood, Timber, Heads, and Barks in **Prior's Wood.**

		l.	*s.*	*d.*
Sold the Underwood to the feveral Perfons mention'd —		339	15	0
Sold the Timber-trees to the feveral Perfons mention'd —		926	8	0
Sold the Heads of the Trees to the feveral Perfons mention'd		123	2	0
Sold the Bark of the Trees to the feveral Perfons mention'd		349	0	10
Total Amount for Underwood, Timber, Heads, and Bark—		1738	5	10

An

An ACCOMPT *of*

Disburſements *or* Out-goings

From the Four ſeveral Manors of G, H, I, K, *in* the County of H, *paid by* A. B. *Steward to His Grace the Duke of* K.

(for one whole Year)

From *Lady-day* 1725 to *Lady-day* 1726.

NB. Every Steward that is curious ſhou'd take particular Care to have *all* his Bills and Vouchers drawn out upon a ſheet or half-ſheet of Paper, according to the bigneſs of the Bill, and to fold them *all* up *exactly* of an equal bigneſs, and to *endorſe* them on the backſide, and alſo to number 'em as to anſwer the N in the following Diſburſements, in the firſt Column. The being exact in this, will make eaſy the examining all ſorts of Accompts.

An Account of Disbursements for the Land-Tax.

		l.	*s.*	*d*
N° 1	Paid Mr. *John Collins* Collector, for the four Quarterly Payments of the Land-Tax, from *Lady-day* 1725 to *Lady-day* 1726, for the Manor of *G*; as appears by his Receipts — — — — —	17	0	0
2	Paid Mr. *John Collins* Collector, for the 4 Quarterly Payments of the Land-Tax, from *Lady-day* 1725 to *Lady-day* 1726, for the Manor of *H*; as appears by his Receipts — — — — —	27	0	0
3	Paid Mr. *John Collins* Collector, for the 4 Quarterly Payments of the Land-Tax, from *Lady-day* 1725 to *Lady-day* 1726, for the Manor of *I*; as appears by his Receipts — — — — —	57	0	0
4	Paid Mr. *John Collins* Collector, for the 4 Quarterly Payments of the Land-Tax, from *Lady-day* 1725 to *Lady-day* 1726, for the Manor of *K*; as appears by his Receipts — — — — —	30	0	0
	Total for the Land-Tax —	131	0	0

Disbursements for the *Church*, *Poor*, and *Constable's* Assessments for Lands in hand.

		l.	*s.*	*d*
5	Paid *John Trolop* Church-warden, for 4 Quarterly Assessments for the *Church* from *Lady-day* 1725 to *Lady-day* 1726, for the Manor *K*. House, Park, land Gardens and Woods in hand — — — — —	4	10	0
6	Paid *Robert Hunt*, for 4 Quarterly Assessments for the *Poor* from *Lady-day* 1725 to *Lady-day* 1726, for *ditto* Lands — — — — —	5	10	0
7	Paid *Thomas Newton*, for 4 Quarterly Assessments for the *Constable* from *Lady-day* 1725 to *Lady-day* 1726, for *ditto* Lands — — — — —	0	10	6
	Total for the Church, Poor, and Constable's Assessments —	10	10	6

Disburse-

Disbursements for the Repairs of several Farm-Houses, by agreement at the time an Improvement in the Manor *K* was made; but for the future there is to be no Allowance made on this account, *all* the Tenants being oblig'd to build and repair at their proper Cost and Charge, they being allow'd rough Timber and Stone to do the same.

N°		*l.*	*s.*	
8	Paid *John Clarke*'s Bill for Masons Work done for *Robert Hunt*, Tenant for the Priory Farm, as appears by his Receipt — — — — — — —	19	15	0
9	Paid *Robert Gefferson*'s Bill for Carpenters Work done for *ditto Hunt* for *ditto* Farm, as appears by his Receipt — — — — — — — —	13	10	0
10	Paid *Thomas Clark*'s Bill for Masons Work done for *John Scot*, Tenant for Ecclefwall Farm, as appears by his Receipt, — — — — —	24	5	0
11	Paid *John Gregory*'s Bill for Carpenters Work done for *ditto Scot* for *ditto* Farm-house, as appears by his Receipt, — — — — — — —	15	10	0
12	Paid *John Scarth*'s Bill for Masons Work done for *John Hill*'s Farm at the Castle, as appears by his Receipt — — — — — — —	34	10	0
13	Paid *Robert Gefferson*'s Bill for Carpenters Work done for *ditto Hill* at *ditto* Farm, as appears by his Receipt, — — — — — — —	19	15	0
14	Paid *John Clarke*'s Bill for Masons Work done for *Richard Bland*, Tenant for Blake's Farm, as appears by his Receipt, — — — — — —	17	0	0
15	Paid *Robert Gregory*'s Bill for Carpenters Work done for *ditto Bland* for *ditto* Farm, as appears by his Receipt, — — — — — —	9	15	0
	Total for Repairs of Farm-Houses —	154	0	0

NB. The Glazier's, &c. Bills were paid by the Tenants by agreement.

Q q

Dis-

Disbursements for repairing and fitting up the Manor-house
  againſt the time Your Grace comes down to look into
  your affairs.

[Done by Your Grace's order.]

Nº		*l.*	*s.*	*d.*
16	PAid *John Clark*'s Bill for Maſons Work done by him in the ſeveral parts of the Houſe, as appears by his Bill and Receipt — — — — —	74	10	0
17	PAid *John Gregory*'s Bill for Carpenters Work done by him in ſeveral parts of the Houſe, as appears by his Bill and Receipt — — — — —	36	0	0
18	PAid *John Cummins*'s Bill for Joyners Work done by him in ſeveral parts of the Houſe, as appears by his Bill and Receipt, — — — — — —	42	0	0
19	PAid *John Blunt*'s Bill for Bricklayers Work done by him in ſeveral parts of the Houſe, as appears by his Bill and Receipt, — — — — —	19	10	0
20	PAid *Jonathan Cox*'s Bill for Glaziers Work done by him in ſeveral parts of the Houſe, as appears by his Bill and Receipt, — — — — —	7	15	0
21	PAid *Jonathan Roberts*'s Bill for Plaiſterers Work done by him in ſeveral parts of the Houſe, as appears by his Bill and Receipt, — — — — —	7	10	0
	Total for repairing the Manor-houſe —	187	5	0

NB. The Bills for Furniture, and putting them up, were paid by the Groom of the Chambers, by your Grace's order.

Dis-

Disbursements for the Repairs and fitting up the Gardens.

[By Your Grace's order]

N°		*l.*	*s.*	*d*
22	Paid *John Blunt*'s Bill for Bricklayers Work done him in building a South-East and South-West Wall, in order to plant the choicest Fruit against the same, as appears by his Bill and Receipt— —	59	10	0
23	Paid *Nicholas Parker*'s Bill the Nursery-man, for several sorts of Fruit-Trees sent from *London,* as appears by his Bill and Receipt, — — — —	23	18	0
24	Paid *John Gregory*'s Bill for Carpenters Work done by him in several parts of the Green-houses, &c. and other Out-houses belonging to the Garden, as appears by his Bill and Receipt — —	15	10	0
25	Paid *Jonathan Cox*'s Bill for Glaziers Work and Glass done by him, for Glass Frames for the Melon-ground, &c. as appears by his Bill and Receipt	8	17	0
26	Paid *John Wyld*'s Bill for Bell-glasses for the use of the several parts of the Kitchen-garden, as appears by his Bill and Receipt — — — — —	2	15	0
27	Paid *John Fletcher* the Gardener's Bill for several Garden-Tools which he bought; also for several sorts of Seeds he bought in *London,* and also for the several Labourers he employ'd in the Gardens, the Particulars of which may be seen in his Accompt, which I have examin'd, — — — — —	73	16	0
	Total for the Garden Accompt—	184	6	0

Disburse-

Disburfements for the feveral forts of Work done in the Park.

		l.	*s.*	*d.*
28	Paid *John Gregory*'s Bill for Carpenters Work done by him, in making Pales to divide the Park into 3 parts, in order to *drive* the Park once a year, as appears by his Bill and Receipt, — — —	175	o	o
29	Paid *John Lacy* the Park-keeper's Bill for the feveral *Labourers* he employ'd in doing odd Jobbs in the Park, and alfo for mowing and making Hay in the Park-bottoms for the ufe of the Deer and Houfe ; all which Particulars appears by his Bill, which I have examin'd, — — —	49	15	6
30	Paid *Robert Clay*'s Bill for Smiths Work done by him, for making new Locks and Keys for the feveral Park-gates, as appears by his Bill and Receipt	3	15	o
31	Paid *John Gregory*'s Bill for Carpenters Work done by him, for making 3 new Swing-gates for the Park, he finding Nails and other Iron-work, as appears by his Bill and Receipt, — — — —	4	15	o
32	Paid *Tho. Bowman*'s Bill for Work done by him in painting the 'foremention'd Gates and other Pales fronting the Manor-houfe, as appears by his Bill and Receipt, — — — — — — — —	6	18	o

Total for the Park Accompt —— 240 3 6

NB. I might have Enter'd more variety of Disburfements, but thefe are fufficient to fhew the Method of being Particular in fuch Accompts. As for Arrears, I have taken no notice of, hoping the Induftrious Steward will make it his Study, for his Lord's Intereft, to prevent them.

Disbursements and Allowances for Salary and Servants-wages.

		l.	*s.*	*d.*
Nº 33	Paid my Self my year's Salary allow'd by Your Grace for collecting the Rents and riding over the whole Estate once a month, to see that the Tenants perform their *Covenants*, and that they manage their Farms to the best advantage, for themselves as well as the Lord of the Manor —	150	0	0
34	Paid Mrs. *Mary Chambers*, the House-keeper, her year's Wages, according to agreement with my Lady Dutchess — — — — — —	15	0	0
35	Paid *Eliz. Cox*, one of the House-Maids, her yearly Wages, according to agreement with the House-keeper, — — — — — —	3	15	0
36	Paid *Jane Long*, the other House-Maid and Dairy-Maid, her yearly Wages, according to agreement with the House-keeper, — — —	3	15	0
37	Paid *John Fletcher* the Gardener his yearly Wages, according to agreement with your Grace,	15	0	0
38	Paid *John Lacy*, the Park-keeper, his yearly Wages according to agreement with your Grace, besides the Perquisites of the Skins, Shoulders, Humbles, Fat, and Ten Shillings Fees for every Buck, and Five Shillings for every Doe kill'd out of the Park, that are sent as *Presents* to Country Gentlemen round, — — — — — — — —	5	0	0
	Total for Servants-wages —	192	10	0

NB. There are several other Disbursements relating to Board-wages, *&c.* that might have been enter'd, but these are sufficient to shew the Method of entering the several Kinds by themselves. The Bills and Vouchers are suppos'd to shew more Particulars, which are to be perused at the time of examining these Accompts.

R r

An

An 𝕬𝖇𝖘𝖙𝖗𝖆𝖈𝖙; or, an 𝕬𝖈𝖈𝖔𝖒𝖕𝖙=𝕮𝖚𝖗𝖗𝖊𝖓𝖙 ſtated going Particulars, in order

From *Lady-day*

A. B. *Steward to His Grace the Duke of* K——, 𝕯𝖊𝖇𝖙𝖔𝖗.	*l.*	*s.*	*d.*
REceiv'd the whole certain Rents from the four ſeveral Manors of *G, H, I, K*; as appears by the Rentals, *Page* 139 — — — — — — —	3525	7	5
REceiv'd the Caſual Profits of Courts by Fines, Hariots, and Surrenders, as appears by that Accompt *p.* 140, 141, — — — — — —	365	8	3
REceiv'd the Three Years Caſual Profits by the Tenants plowing up freſh Paſture-Land, as appears by that Accompt *p.* 142, — — — —	492	12	6
REceiv'd for the Sale of the Underwood, Timber-Trees, Heads, and Bark, in 𝕻𝖗𝖎𝖔𝖗'𝖘 𝖂𝖔𝖔𝖉 in the Manor of *K*, as appears by that Accompt *p.* 143, 144, 145, 146 — — — — — — —	1738	5	10
Total of what I have receiv'd — *L.*	6121	14	0

y of *Debtor* and *Creditor* from all the 'fore-
ew the exact Balance:

Lady-day 1726.

per *Contra* — — — — **Creditor.**	*l.*	*s.*	*d.*
PAid the four Quarterly Payments of the Land-Tax for the Manors of *G, H, I, K*; as appears by that Accompt, *Page* 148 — — — — — —	131	0	0
PAid the 4 Quarterly Affeffments for the *Church*, *Poor*, and *Conftable*, for the Manor of *K* Houfe, Park, and Gardens, and Woods kept in hand; as appears by that Accompt *p.* 148, — — — — —	10	10	6
PAid the feveral Bills for the Repairs of the feveral Farm-houfes by agreement, as appears by that Accompt *p.* 149 — — — — — — — — —	154	0	0
PAid the feveral Bills for repairing and fitting up the Manor-Houfe againft the time your Grace comes down to look into your affairs; done by your Grace's Order, *p.* 150 — — — — — — — —	187	5	0
PAid the feveral Bills for the Repairs and fitting up the Gardens, by your Grace's order, *p.* 151 — —	184	6	0
PAid the feveral Bills for the feveral forts of Work done in the Park, as appears by thofe Accompts, *p.* 152 — — — — — — — — — —	240	3	6
PAid the feveral Servants-wages, as appears by that Accompt and Vouchers, *p.* 153 — — — — —	192	10	0
Total Disburfements —	1099	15	0
REturn'd and paid to *John Mead* Efq; your Grace's Banker, by feveral Bills, as will appear by his Accompt, to balance this whole years Accompt from *Lady-day* 1725 to *Lady-day* 1726,— — — — —	5021	19	0
Total of what I have paid —*L.*	6121	14	0

This is a True Accompt, (Errors excepted) witnefs my Hand,

A. B

A particular Account of the

Prices of the several Artificers Works

Which relate to

Ordinary Buildings, and the Repairs of Farm-Houses, Mills, &c.

ALSO

The Prices of the several sorts of *Works* relating to *Husbandry*, computed according to *Labourers Wages* in most Parts of the *North*, at Twelve-pence a Day in *Summer*, and Nine-pence in the *Winter*.

NB. As Labourers Wages are something more in the South of ENGLAND, and something less in the more Northern parts, so 'tis easy for every Steward to adjust a Price in proportion to Labourers Wages in the several parts.

Also if any new sort of Work is to be done, not mention'd in the following Particulars, the Steward's best way is to hire a good Labourer, and to stand by him the whole Day, to see that he does a good Days-Work, and then to measure the same, in order to know what it is worth.

The Prices of Ordinary Buildings, and Repairs of Farm - Houses *in the Northern parts of* England.

NB. A Rod is suppos'd to contain 21 foot in length, which is the Dimensions in most parts of the *North* ; but if in other parts of *England* the customary Rod shou'd be more or less, then the Rule of Proportion must be used.

'Tis also suppos'd that all Materials are found, and laid at hand for the Workmen, (except the Glazier's) which is *much* the best way, because the Workmen sometimes are apt to *impose* and use bad Materials.

Masons Work.

HAmmér'd Double-walling 22 Inches thick, of middling Freestone, containing a Rod in length; and 3 Foot high, which is call'd a Rod of *Masons Work*, may be done for 5 s. 6 d.

Coarse Flagging of the 'foremention'd Stone, being rough hammer'd, may be done for 1 s. 4 d. a superficial Yard.

Door-Jaumes and Window-Jaumes, of Hewn-work of the 'foremention'd Stone, may be done for 3 *d*. a superficial Foot.

The Price for carrying up Chimneys is conformable to the height of the Building; which, if of a middling height, may be done for about 5 *s*. a Story for each Chimney, and 3 *d*. a Foot for the Chimney-tops of hewn Stone.

Paving-work of Flint or Pebble-stones for Stables or Court-yards, &c. may be done for 2 *d*. half-penny a superficial Yard.

Bricklayers Work.

WALLS of a Brick in length may be done for 2 *s*. a Rod.

Walls of a Brick and half may be done for 2 *s*. 10 *d*. a Rod.

Partition-walls a Brick in breadth, which often are used in low Houses, may be done for 1 *s*. 6 *d*. a Rod.

Lathing, Tyling, and pointing the Tyles, may be done for 6 *d*. a Rod.

Plai-

Plaiſtering the inſides of Brick or Stone-walls with Lime and Hair, two Coats, the one coarſe, the other fine, may be done for 2 *d.* a Yard; but if plaiſter'd with three Coats, the Price is 3 *d.* a Yard.

Lathing and Plaiſtering for Ceiling-Staircaſes may be done for 4 *d.* a Yard.

NB.   Seven hundred Bricks will make a Rod of Walling of a Brick thick; and ſo in proportion for every thickneſs.

In digging Foundations, the Price is according to the nature of the Earth : If upon a Rock, it will coſt 6 *d.* a ſolid Yard; but if upon a Clay or other light Soil, it may be done for 4 *d.* a ſolid Yard.

Carpenters Work.

ROOFING for plain Tyling, may be done for 6 *d.* a Square, *i. e.* One hundred ſquare Feet.

Flooring with Joyce and Dorments; and laying the Floors, which is call'd Double Meaſure, may be done for 12 *s.* a Square.

Single

Single Posts and Rails for securing Quick-wood, may be done for 4 *d.* a Rod running measure.

Plain Wainscotting, and making Doors and Windows, may be done for 1 *s.* 6 *d.* a superficial Yard.

Park-paling eight foot high, with Posts and three Rails, may be done for 12 *d.* a Yard running measure, or 7 *s.* a Rod.

Glaziers Work.

COmmon Windows (with *Newcastle* or *Sunderland* Glass) the Glazier finding Glass, Lead, and *all* other Materials, may be done for 5 *d.* a Foot.

Mill-

Millwrights Work.

BEcause *over-shot* Water-Mills are become most general, (especially in the Northern parts of *England*) and indeed do the least hurt to the Publick, (as they are generally placed) I shall in the first place give the Prices as perform'd by Mr. *Ralph Fowler*, Millwright to the Right Honourable the Earl of *Carlisle*, at *Castle-Howard* in *York-shire*. If other Noblemen or Gentlemen are pleas'd to employ him, I am satisfied they will be faithfully serv'd at reasonable rates.

For making a Water-wheel, 4 pounds.
For making a Cogg-wheel, 2 pounds.
For making the Axletree, 1 pound.
For Flooring a pair of new Mill-stones, 2 pounds.

NB. I have given these Particulars in case of Repairs, where any one is wanting to be made new.

An *over-shot* Water-Mill (and making all the Utensils belonging) which takes water about the centre of the Axletree, may be built for about 25 pounds, for the Millwright's work only : As for the Roofing, *&c.* which comes under the head of Carpenters and Masons work, 'tis already given in the 'foregoing Pages.

T t   A

A *Windmill* (with all the Utenſils belonging) for grinding Corn may be made for about 30 pounds, for the Millwright's work only.

An *Horſe-Mill* for grinding Malt and ſhelling Oates may be made for about 8 pounds for the Millwright's work only.

Becauſe the *blue* Stones from *Holland* are become moſt general, they being *cheaper*, on the account of laſting 40 or 50 years, I ſhall give the Prices as they are commonly ſold at the Sea-ſide upon the *Northern* Coaſts, according to the ſeveral Dimenſions following.

Inches diameter.	Inches thick.	l.	s.	d.	
54	15	at 20	0	0	a pair.
48	14	at 15	0	0	a pair.
46 and	13	at 11	10	0	a pair.
44	13	at 10	10	0	a pair.
40	12	at 8	10	0	a pair.

For the ſake of ſuch as are not willing to go to the Price of the above-mention'd *blue* Stones, it may not be amiſs to give the Prices of the *grey* Stones, as they are ſold at *Bautry* in *York-ſhire*, according to the ſeveral Dimenſions following.

	l.	s.	d.	
20 hands diameter — — at	11	10	0	a pair.
19 ditto — — — — — at	10	0	0	a pair.
18 ditto — — — — — at	9	0	0	a pair.
17 ditto — — — — — at	8	0	0	a pair.
16 ditto — — — — — at	7	0	0	a pair,
15 ditto — — — — — at	6	0	0	a pair.
14 ditto — — — — — at	5	0	0	a pair.

NB. The Hand is 3¼ Inches.

Works

Works relating to Husbandry.

H Edging, Ditching, and planting double rows of white-Thorn Quickſetts, may be done for 3 pence a Rod running meaſure.

NB. 150 Plants will plant a Rod, which will coſt about 4 Shillings a Thouſand, if rais'd from Berries, which are much the beſt.

For plaſhing a Hedge in the beſt manner, and alſo ditching along the ſame, may be done for 7 *d.* a Rod.

For digging a Ditch ten foot wide at top, and ſix foot wide at the bottom, and four foot deep, (which Dimenſions is commonly practis'd in the Marſhes and Fenns) 2 *s.* a Rod.

Plowing the firſt time on a ſtiff Clay Stubble, may be done for 3 *s.* 6 *d.* an Acre.
Plowing the ſecond time the 'foreſaid Land at 2 *s.* 9 *d.* an Acre.
Plowing, harrowing, and ſowing the third time the 'foreſaid Land, at 3 *s.* 9 *d.* an Acre.

Plowing the firſt time on a light gravelly Soil, at 2 *s.* 9 *d.* per Acre.
Plowing the ſecond time of the 'foreſaid Land, at 2 *s.* 4 *d.* an Acre.
Plowing, harrowing, and ſowing the third time on the aforeſaid Lands, at 3 *s.* per Acre.

Plow-

Plowing the firſt time on a light ſandy Soil, at 2 *s.* an Acre.

Plowing the ſecond time on the aforeſaid Lands, at 1 *s.* 10 *d.* an Acre.

Plowing, harrowing, and ſowing the third time on *ditto* Lands, at 2 *s.* 6 *d.* an Acre.

Reaping and binding of Wheat and Rye may be done for 4 *s.* an Acre.

Mowing of Barley, Oates, and cocking and raking with a Sweath-rake, at 3 *s. per* Acre.

Mowing, raking, and cocking of Hay in Meadows where 'tis pretty rank, at 3 *s.* an Acre.

Mowing, raking, and cocking of Hay in Uplands, where 'tis pretty thin, at 2 *s.* 6 *d.* an Acre.

Thraſhing and winnowing of *Wheat* or *Rye* may be done for 2 *s.* 8 *d.* a quarter.

Thraſhing and winnowing of *Barley*, at 1 *s.* 10 *d.* a quarter.

Thraſhing and winnowing of *Oates*, at 1 *s.* 6 *d.* a quarter.

Thraſhing and winnowing of *Beans* and *Peaſe*, at 2 *s.* a quarter.

A

A
New and Concise Table

OF THE

Solid Measure of *Timber, Stone*, &c.

ready cast up in Feet and Tenths of a Foot, to the greatest
exactness possible in the first place of DECIMALS, answering to every half-Inch from 3 Inches to 75, for the
Fourth part of the Girt, (which in Round Timber is custo-
marily taken as a Side of the Square) and from 1 Foot to
45 in length ; with an Explanation of its Use in several
Cases, shewing how to take readily the Quantity answering to any length of Feet, and Tenths of a Foot, under
46 Foot long : Very easy to be understood by any Person the least conversant in Numbers.

U u   THE

The Explanation and Use of the following Table.

CASE I. THere is a piece of round Timber whose 4th part of the Girt is 18 Inches, and length 32 Feet: Look for 18 in the top Column, under which, even with 32 in the left-hand Column, is 72 Feet for the solid Content.

NB. If it had been squared Timber of 18 Inches each side, the Solution would be the Geome-trical Truth. *Note also,* This first Case is agreeable to the Custom of general Use in measu-ring Timber, *viz.* to reckon the Length only to even Feet, and to half an Inch in the 4th part of the Girt, and the Quantity but to a quarter of a Foot; therefore to have this Table answer thereto, 1 or 2 in the Tenths place may be neglected, 3 or 4 may be express'd $\frac{1}{4}$; 5, 6, or 7, $\frac{1}{2}$; and 8 or 9, $\frac{3}{4}$ of a Foot: But for such as would be more exact, I proceed.

CASE II. There is a piece of Timber whose fourth part of the Girt is 18 Inches, and length 32.4 Feet; then look, as above, for the quantity answering 32 Foot long, but for the .4 equal to $\frac{4}{10}$ of a Foot look down in the same 18 inches Co-lumn for the quantity even with 4 in the left-hand Column, which you will find to be 9 feet, but must be made .9 equal to $\frac{9}{10}$ of a solid foot, which in this Case may be placed thus:

$$32.0 \text{ Feet in length is} \text{---} 72.0$$
$$.4 \text{ equal to } \tfrac{4}{10} \text{ of a Foot is} \text{---} .9 \Big\} \text{ solid Feet.}$$
$$32.4 \text{ equal to } 32\tfrac{4}{10} \text{ Feet is} \text{---} 72.9$$

72	.0
72	.9
141	.9
630	.1
144	.0
204	.0
226	.9
592	.1
2083	.9

NB. That those who do not understand *Decimal Fractions* in general, may understand those in this Table, I think proper not only to mention, that any Figure placed on the right-hand of a Point denotes it to be Tenths of an Integer, as .1 is $\frac{1}{10}$, .2 is $\frac{2}{10}$, &c. therefore .9 added to 72 Feet, will be 72.9, equal to $72\frac{9}{10}$ Feet; but also to place in the Margin the Solu-tions of these several Cases, with their Sum-Total, as a Specimen to shew the manner of their Addition, which is the same as whole Numbers.

CASE III. There is a piece of Timber to be measur'd of 37 foot long, which is taper, (*i. e.* bigger at one end than the other) the custom is to take the Girt at the middle; then look as before in the top Column for $\frac{1}{4}$ of the Girt, which suppose $23\frac{1}{4}$ inches, and below, even with 37, is 141.9 solid feet for the quantity.

NB. This Table is continued to so great a space for one fourth of the Girt, that the quantity of *Stone* or *Marble-blocks* (which are often very large) may be taken out at once, they being generally hewn out in the rough not much differing in form from a piece of squared Timber, and if a Stone or Marble-block should be in form of a *Parallelopipedon,* 'tis customary to take a Mean between the Dimension of the two Sides, as a Side of the Square, whereby the quan-tity is given near enough, unless the two Sides are much different from one another.

CASE

CASE IV. There is a Stone or Marble-block in form of a *Parallelopipedon*, whose one side is 69, t'other 73 inches, and 18 foot long; to find the mean side add 69 & 73 together, the sum is 142, half whereof is the mean side, *viz.* 71, which look for in the top Column, and below even with 18 the length in feet is 630.1 feet for the quantity, which differs *little* from the truth.

CASE V. There is a Stone or Marble-block in form of a *Parallelopipedon*, whose one side is 24, t'other 72 inches, and 12 foot long; here the mean side would be 48, under which even with 12 is 192 feet for the quantity, which is a deal too much. *NB.* In this Case it is necessary to enquire how many times 24 is in 72, which being 3 times, it may be suppos'd three Stones of 24 inches for a Side of the Square, and 12 foot long; or else one Stone of 3 times that length, (*i. e.* 36 foot long) whose quantity is but 144 feet.

CASE VI. There is a Stone or Marble-block in form of a *Parallelopipedon*, whose one side is 23, t'other 75 inches, and length 17 feet; here a third part of 75 is 25, and the mean between 23 & 25 is 24, which must be taken, and the Stone counted 3 Stones; then under 24, even with 17, is 68 feet for quantity of each, which *multiplied* by 3, make 204 for the whole.

CASE VII. There is a Stone or Marble-block in form of a *Parallelopipedon*, whose one side is 36, t'other 60 inches, and 15 foot long; here half 60 is 30, and a mean between 30 & 36 is 33, which may be taken, and the length suppos'd double, *viz.* 30 feet; then under 33, even with 30, is 226.9 feet for quantity. *NB.* The best way in this Case would be to suppose it one Stone of 60 inches for a side of the Square, and thrice 36 inches long, *viz.* 9 feet, because 60 inches measures at thrice exactly 15 feet; thus the quantity would be but 225 feet, which is the Geometrical truth.

CASE VIII. There is a Stone whose every side is unequal, or it may be near to round; the custom is to gird it as Timber, and take a 4th of it, which suppose 73 inches, and length 16 feet; under 73, even with the length, is 592.1 f. the quantity. *NB.* In measuring *Timber, Stone,* &c. 'tis convenient to have a ten-foot Rod in 2 parts, which can slide in to 5 Feet, divided into Feet and Tenths throughout; but in measuring Timber standing, 'tis sufficient to have a very long Pole divided into Feet only (beside a pocket Foot-Rule divided into Inches) and a Ladder to get up with readily, to measure the Girt of the Tree at the middle height to which it runs Timber; and if the Tree to be measur'd is an old thick-bark'd Tree, something considerable must be abated in a fourth part of the Girt for the Bark; but in young growing Timber half an Inch may be sufficient.

The

Len. in Feet	The Fourth part of the Girt in Inches.															
	3	3½	4	4½	5	5½	6	6½	7	7½	8	8½	9	9½	10	10½
1	.1	.1	.1	.1	.2	.2	.3	.3	.3	.4	.4	.5	.6	.6	.7	
2	.1	.2	.2	.3	.3	.4	.5	.6	.7	.8	.9	1.0	1.1	1.3	1.4	1.
3	.2	.3	.3	.4	.5	.6	.8	.9	1.0	1.2	1.3	1.5	1.7	1.9	2.1	2.
4	.3	.3	.4	.6	.7	.8	1.0	1.2	1.4	1.6	1.8	2.0	2.3	2.5	2.8	3
5	.3	.4	.6	.7	.9	1.1	1.3	1.5	1.7	2.0	2.2	2.5	2.8	3.1	3.5	3
6	.4	.5	.7	.8	1.0	1.3	1.5	1.8	2.0	2.3	2.7	3.0	3.4	3.8	4.2	4
7	.4	.6	.8	1.0	1.2	1.5	1.8	2.1	2.4	2.7	3.1	3.5	3.9	4.4	4.9	5
8	.5	.7	.9	1.1	1.4	1.7	2.0	2.3	2.7	3.1	3.6	4.0	4.5	5.0	5.6	6
9	.6	.8	1.0	1.3	1.6	1.9	2.3	2.6	3.1	3.5	4.0	4.5	5.1	5.6	6.3	6
10	.6	.9	1.1	1.4	1.7	2.1	2.5	2.9	3.4	3.9	4.4	5.0	5.6	6.3	6.9	7
11	.7	.9	1.2	1.5	1.9	2.3	2.8	3.2	3.7	4.3	4.9	5.5	6.2	6.9	7.6	8
12	.8	1.0	1.3	1.7	2.1	2.5	3.0	3.5	4.1	4.7	5.3	6.0	6.8	7.5	8.3	9
13	.8	1.1	1.4	1.8	2.3	2.7	3.3	3.8	4.4	5.1	5.8	6.5	7.3	8.1	9.0	10
14	.9	1.2	1.6	2.0	2.4	2.9	3.5	4.1	4.8	5.5	6.2	7.0	7.9	8.8	9.7	10
15	.9	1.3	1.7	2.1	2.6	3.2	3.8	4.4	5.1	5.9	6.7	7.5	8.4	9.4	10.4	11
16	1.0	1.4	1.8	2.3	2.8	3.4	4.0	4.7	5.4	6.3	7.1	8.0	9.0	10.0	11.1	12
17	1.1	1.4	1.9	2.4	3.0	3.6	4.3	5.0	5.8	6.6	7.6	8.5	9.6	10.6	11.8	13
18	1.1	1.5	2.0	2.5	3.1	3.8	4.5	5.3	6.1	7.0	8.0	9.0	10.1	11.3	12.5	13
19	1.2	1.6	2.1	2.7	3.3	4.0	4.8	5.6	6.5	7.4	8.4	9.5	10.7	11.9	13.2	14
20	1.3	1.7	2.2	2.8	3.5	4.2	5.0	5.9	6.8	7.8	8.9	10.0	11.2	12.5	13.9	15
21	1.3	1.8	2.3	3.0	3.6	4.4	5.3	6.2	7.1	8.2	9.3	10.5	11.8	13.2	14.6	16
22	1.4	1.9	2.4	3.1	3.8	4.6	5.5	6.5	7.5	8.6	9.8	11.0	12.4	13.8	15.3	16
23	1.4	2.0	2.6	3.2	4.0	4.8	5.8	6.7	7.8	9.0	10.2	11.5	12.9	14.4	16.0	17
24	1.5	2.0	2.7	3.4	4.2	5.0	6.0	7.0	8.2	9.4	10.7	12.0	13.5	15.0	16.7	18
25	1.6	2.1	2.8	3.5	4.3	5.3	6.3	7.3	8.5	9.8	11.1	12.5	14.1	15.7	17.4	19
26	1.6	2.2	2.9	3.7	4.5	5.5	6.5	7.6	8.8	10.2	11.6	13.0	14.6	16.3	18.1	19
27	1.7	2.3	3.0	3.8	4.7	5.7	6.8	7.9	9.2	10.5	12.0	13.5	15.2	16.9	18.8	20
28	1.8	2.4	3.1	3.9	4.9	5.9	7.0	8.2	9.5	10.9	12.4	14.0	15.8	17.5	19.4	21
29	1.8	2.5	3.2	4.1	5.0	6.1	7.3	8.5	9.9	11.3	12.9	14.6	16.3	18.2	20.1	22
30	1.9	2.6	3.3	4.2	5.2	6.3	7.5	8.8	10.2	11.7	13.3	15.1	16.9	18.8	20.8	23
31	1.9	2.6	3.4	4.4	5.4	6.5	7.8	9.1	10.5	12.1	13.8	15.6	17.4	19.4	21.5	23
32	2.0	2.7	3.6	4.5	5.6	6.7	8.0	9.4	10.9	12.5	14.2	16.1	18.0	20.1	22.2	24
33	2.1	2.8	3.7	4.6	5.7	6.9	8.3	9.7	11.2	12.9	14.7	16.6	18.6	20.7	22.9	25
34	2.1	2.9	3.8	4.8	5.9	7.1	8.5	10.0	11.6	13.3	15.1	17.1	19.1	21.3	23.6	26
35	2.2	3.0	3.9	4.9	6.1	7.4	8.8	10.3	11.9	13.7	15.6	17.6	19.7	21.9	24.3	26
36	2.3	3.1	4.0	5.1	6.3	7.6	9.0	10.6	12.3	14.1	16.0	18.1	20.3	22.6	25.0	27
37	2.3	3.1	4.1	5.2	6.4	7.8	9.3	10.9	12.6	14.5	16.4	18.6	20.8	23.2	25.7	28
38	2.4	3.2	4.2	5.3	6.6	8.0	9.5	11.1	12.9	14.8	16.9	19.1	21.4	23.8	26.4	29
39	2.4	3.3	4.3	5.5	6.8	8.2	9.8	11.4	13.3	15.2	17.3	19.6	21.9	24.4	27.1	39
40	2.5	3.4	4.4	5.6	6.9	8.4	10.0	11.7	13.6	15.6	17.8	20.1	22.5	25.1	27.8	30
41	2.6	3.5	4.6	5.8	7.1	8.6	10.3	12.0	14.0	16.0	18.2	20.6	23.1	25.7	28.5	31
42	2.6	3.6	4.7	5.9	7.3	8.8	10.5	12.3	14.3	16.4	18.7	21.1	23.6	26.3	29.2	32
43	2.7	3.7	4.8	6.0	7.5	9.0	10.8	12.6	14.6	16.8	19.1	21.6	24.2	26.9	29.9	32
44	2.8	3.7	4.9	6.2	7.6	9.2	11.0	12.9	15.0	17.2	19.6	22.1	24.8	27.6	30.6	33
45	2.8	3.8	5.0	6.3	7.8	9.5	11.3	13.2	15.3	17.6	20.0	22.6	25.3	28.2	31.3	34

The Fourth part of the Girt in Inches.

11	11½	12	12½	13	13½	14	14½	15	15½	16	16½	17	17½	18	18½
.8	.9	1.0	1.1	1.2	1.3	1.4	1.5	1.6	1.7	1.8	1.9	2.0	2.1	2.3	2.4
1.7	1.8	2.0	2.2	2.3	2.5	2.7	2.9	3.1	3.3	3.6	3.8	4.0	4.2	4.5	4.8
2.5	2.8	3.0	3.3	3.5	3.8	4.1	4.4	4.7	5.0	5.3	5.7	6.0	6.4	6.8	7.1
3.4	3.7	4.0	4.3	4.7	5.1	5.4	5.8	6.3	6.7	7.1	7.6	8.0	8.5	9.0	9.5
4.2	4.6	5.0	5.4	5.9	6.3	6.8	7.3	7.8	8.3	8.9	9.5	10.0	10.6	11.3	11.9
5.0	5.5	6.0	6.5	7.0	7.6	8.2	8.8	9.4	10.0	10.7	11.3	12.0	12.8	13.5	14.3
5.9	6.4	7.0	7.6	8.2	8.9	9.5	10.2	10.9	11.7	12.4	13.2	14.0	14.9	15.8	16.6
6.7	7.3	8.0	8.7	9.4	10.1	10.9	11.7	12.5	13.3	14.2	15.1	16.1	17.0	18.0	19.0
7.6	8.3	9.0	9.8	10.6	11.4	12.3	13.1	14.1	15.0	16.0	17.0	18.1	19.1	20.3	21.4
8.4	9.2	10.0	10.9	11.7	12.7	13.6	14.6	15.6	16.7	17.8	18.9	20.1	21.3	22.5	23.8
9.2	10.1	11.0	11.9	12.9	13.9	15.0	16.1	17.2	18.4	19.6	20.8	22.1	23.4	24.8	26.1
10.1	11.0	12.0	13.0	14.1	15.2	16.3	17.5	18.8	20.0	21.3	22.7	24.1	25.5	27.0	28.5
10.9	11.9	13.0	14.1	15.3	16.5	17.7	19.0	20.3	21.7	23.1	24.6	26.1	27.6	29.3	30.9
11.8	12.9	14.0	15.2	16.4	17.7	19.1	20.4	21.9	23.4	24.9	26.5	28.1	29.8	31.5	33.3
12.6	13.8	15.0	16.3	17.6	19.0	20.4	21.9	23.4	25.0	26.7	28.4	30.1	31.9	33.8	35.7
13.4	14.7	16.0	17.4	18.8	20.3	21.8	23.4	25.0	26.7	28.4	30.3	32.1	34.0	36.0	38.0
14.3	15.6	17.0	18.4	20.0	21.5	23.1	24.8	26.6	28.4	30.2	32.1	34.1	36.2	38.3	40.4
15.1	16.5	18.0	19.5	21.1	22.8	24.5	26.3	28.1	30.0	32.0	34.0	36.1	38.3	40.5	42.8
16.0	17.4	19.0	20.6	22.3	24.0	25.9	27.7	29.7	31.7	33.8	35.9	38.1	40.4	42.8	45.2
16.8	18.4	20.0	21.7	23.5	25.3	27.2	29.2	31.3	33.4	35.6	37.8	40.1	42.5	45.0	47.5
17.6	19.3	21.0	22.8	24.6	26.6	28.6	30.7	32.8	35.0	37.3	39.7	42.1	44.7	47.3	49.9
18.5	20.2	22.0	23.9	25.8	27.8	29.9	32.1	34.4	36.7	39.1	41.6	44.2	46.8	49.5	52.3
19.3	21.1	23.0	25.0	27.0	29.1	31.3	33.6	35.9	38.4	40.9	43.5	46.2	48.9	51.8	54.7
20.2	22.0	24.0	26.0	28.2	30.4	32.7	35.0	37.5	40.0	42.7	45.4	48.2	51.0	54.0	57.0
21.0	23.0	25.0	27.1	29.3	31.6	34.0	36.5	39.1	41.7	44.4	47.3	50.2	53.2	56.3	59.4
21.8	23.9	26.0	28.2	30.5	32.9	35.4	38.0	40.6	43.4	46.2	49.2	52.2	55.3	58.5	61.8
22.7	24.8	27.0	29.3	31.7	34.2	36.8	39.4	42.2	45.0	48.0	51.0	54.2	57.4	60.8	64.2
23.5	25.7	28.0	30.4	32.9	35.4	38.1	40.9	43.8	46.7	49.8	52.9	56.2	59.5	63.0	66.5
24.4	26.6	29.0	31.5	34.0	36.7	39.5	42.3	45.3	48.4	51.6	54.8	58.2	61.7	65.3	68.9
25.2	27.6	30.0	32.6	35.2	38.0	40.8	43.8	46.9	50.1	53.3	56.7	60.2	63.8	67.5	71.3
26.0	28.5	31.0	33.6	36.4	39.2	42.2	45.3	48.4	51.7	55.1	58.6	62.2	65.9	69.8	73.7
26.9	29.4	32.0	34.7	37.6	40.5	43.6	46.7	50.0	53.4	56.9	60.5	64.2	68.1	72.0	76.1
27.7	30.3	33.0	35.8	38.7	41.8	44.9	48.2	51.6	55.1	58.7	62.4	66.2	70.2	74.3	78.4
28.6	31.2	34.0	36.9	39.9	43.0	46.3	49.6	53.1	56.7	60.4	64.3	68.2	72.4	76.5	80.8
29.4	32.1	35.0	38.0	41.1	44.3	47.6	51.1	54.7	58.4	62.2	66.2	70.2	74.4	78.8	83.2
30.3	33.1	36.0	39.1	42.3	45.6	49.0	52.6	56.3	60.1	64.0	68.1	72.3	76.6	81.0	85.6
31.1	34.0	37.0	40.1	43.4	46.8	50.4	54.0	57.8	61.7	65.8	70.0	74.3	78.7	83.3	87.9
31.9	34.9	38.0	41.2	44.6	48.1	51.7	55.5	59.4	63.4	67.6	71.8	76.3	80.8	85.5	90.3
32.8	35.8	39.0	42.3	45.8	49.4	53.1	56.9	60.9	65.1	69.3	73.7	78.3	82.9	87.8	92.7
33.6	36.7	40.0	43.4	46.9	50.6	54.4	58.4	62.5	66.7	71.1	75.6	80.3	85.1	90.0	95.1
34.5	37.7	41.0	44.5	48.1	51.9	55.8	59.9	64.1	68.4	72.9	77.5	82.3	87.2	92.3	97.4
35.3	38.6	42.0	45.6	49.3	53.2	57.2	61.3	65.6	70.1	74.7	79.4	84.3	89.3	94.5	99.8
36.1	39.5	43.0	46.7	50.5	54.4	58.5	62.8	67.2	71.7	76.4	81.3	86.3	91.4	96.8	102.2
37.0	40.4	44.0	47.7	51.6	55.7	59.9	64.2	68.8	73.4	78.2	83.2	88.3	93.6	99.0	104.6
37.8	41.3	45.0	48.8	52.8	57.0	61.3	65.7	70.3	75.1	80.0	85.1	90.3	95.7	101.3	107.0

X x

The

Len. in Feet	The Fourth part of the Girt in Inches.													
	19	19½	20	20½	21	21¼	22	22½	23	23½	24	24½	25	25
1	2.5	2.6	2.8	2.9	3.1	3.2	3.4	3.5	3.7	3.8	4.0	4.2	4.3	4
2	5.0	5.3	5.6	5.8	6.1	6.4	6.7	7.0	7.3	7.7	8.0	8.3	8.7	9
3	7.5	7.9	8.3	8.8	9.2	9.6	10.1	10.5	11.0	11.5	12.0	12.5	13.0	13
4	10.0	10.6	11.1	11.7	12.3	12.8	13.4	14.1	14.7	15.3	16.0	16.7	17.4	18
5	12.5	13.2	13.9	14.6	15.3	16.1	16.8	17.6	18.4	19.2	20.0	20.8	21.7	22
6	15.0	15.8	16.7	17.5	18.4	19.3	20.2	21.1	22.0	23.0	24.0	25.0	26.0	—
7	17.5	18.5	19.4	20.4	21.4	22.5	23.5	24.6	25.7	26.8	28.0	29.2	30.4	27
8	20.1	21.1	22.2	23.3	24.5	25.7	26.9	28.1	29.4	30.7	32.0	33.3	34.7	36
9	22.6	23.8	25.0	26.3	27.6	28.9	30.3	31.6	33.1	34.5	36.0	37.5	39.1	40
10	25.1	26.4	27.8	29.2	30.6	32.1	33.6	35.2	36.7	38.4	40.0	41.7	43.4	45
11	27.6	29.0	30.6	32.1	33.7	35.3	37.0	38.7	40.4	42.2	44.0	45.9	47.7	49
12	30.1	31.7	33.3	35.0	36.8	38.5	40.3	42.2	44.1	46.0	48.0	50.0	52.1	54
13	32.6	34.3	36.1	37.9	39.8	41.7	43.7	45.7	47.8	49.9	52.0	54.2	56.4	58
14	35.1	37.0	38.9	40.9	42.9	44.9	47.1	49.2	51.4	53.7	56.0	58.4	60.8	63
15	37.6	39.6	41.7	43.8	45.9	48.2	50.4	52.7	55.1	57.5	60.0	62.5	65.1	67
16	40.1	42.3	44.4	46.7	49.0	51.4	53.8	56.3	58.8	61.4	64.0	66.7	69.4	72
17	42.6	44.9	47.2	49.6	52.1	54.6	57.1	59.8	62.5	65.2	68.0	70.9	73.8	76
18	45.1	47.5	50.0	52.5	55.1	57.8	60.5	63.3	66.1	69.0	72.0	75.0	78.1	81
19	47.6	50.2	52.8	55.4	58.2	61.0	63.9	66.8	69.8	72.9	76.0	79.2	82.5	85
20	50.1	52.8	55.6	58.4	61.3	64.2	67.2	70.3	73.5	76.7	80.0	83.4	86.8	90
21	52.6	55.5	58.3	61.3	64.3	67.4	70.6	73.8	77.1	80.5	84.0	87.5	91.1	94
22	55.2	58.1	61.1	64.2	67.4	70.6	73.9	77.3	80.8	84.4	88.0	91.7	95.5	99
23	57.7	60.7	63.9	67.1	70.4	73.8	77.3	80.9	84.5	88.2	92.0	95.9	99.8	103
24	60.2	63.4	66.7	70.0	73.5	77.0	80.7	84.4	88.2	92.0	96.0	100.0	104.2	108
25	62.7	66.0	69.4	73.0	76.6	80.3	84.0	87.9	91.8	95.9	100.0	104.2	108.5	112
26	65.2	68.7	72.2	75.9	79.6	83.5	87.4	91.4	95.5	99.7	104.0	108.4	112.8	117
27	67.7	71.3	75.0	78.8	82.7	86.7	90.8	94.9	99.2	103.5	108.0	112.5	117.2	121
28	70.2	73.9	77.8	81.7	85.8	89.9	94.1	98.4	102.9	107.4	112.0	116.7	121.5	126
29	72.7	76.6	80.6	84.6	88.8	93.1	97.5	102.0	106.5	111.2	116.0	120.9	125.9	131
30	75.2	79.2	83.3	87.6	91.9	96.3	100.8	105.5	110.2	115.1	120.0	125.1	130.2	135
31	77.7	81.9	86.1	90.5	94.9	99.5	104.2	109.0	113.9	118.9	124.0	129.2	134.5	140
32	80.2	84.5	88.9	93.4	98.0	102.7	107.6	112.5	117.6	122.7	128.0	133.4	138.9	144
33	82.7	87.1	91.7	96.3	101.1	105.9	110.9	116.0	121.2	126.6	132.0	137.6	143.2	149
34	85.2	89.8	94.4	99.2	104.1	109.1	114.3	119.5	124.9	130.4	136.0	141.7	147.6	153
35	87.7	92.4	97.2	102.1	107.2	112.4	117.6	123.0	128.6	134.2	140.0	145.9	151.9	158
36	90.3	95.1	100.0	105.1	110.3	115.6	121.0	126.6	132.3	138.1	144.0	150.1	156.3	162
37	92.8	97.7	102.8	108.0	113.3	118.8	124.4	130.1	135.9	141.9	148.0	154.2	160.6	167
38	95.3	100.3	105.6	110.9	116.4	122.0	127.7	133.6	139.6	145.7	152.0	158.4	164.9	171
39	97.8	103.0	108.3	113.8	119.4	125.2	131.1	137.1	143.3	149.6	156.0	162.6	169.3	176
40	100.3	105.6	111.1	116.7	122.5	128.4	134.4	140.6	146.9	153.4	160.0	166.7	173.6	180
41	102.8	108.3	113.9	119.7	125.6	131.6	137.8	144.1	150.6	157.2	164.0	170.9	178.0	185
42	105.3	110.9	116.7	122.6	128.6	134.8	141.2	147.7	154.3	161.1	168.0	175.1	182.3	189
43	107.8	113.5	119.4	125.5	131.7	138.0	144.5	151.2	158.0	164.9	172.0	179.2	186.6	194
44	110.3	116.2	122.2	128.4	134.8	141.2	147.9	154.7	161.6	168.7	176.0	183.4	191.0	198
45	112.8	118.8	125.0	131.3	137.8	144.5	151.3	158.2	165.3	172.6	180.0	187.6	195.3	203

The Fourth part of the Girt in Inches.

Feet	26	26½	27	27½	28	28½	29	29½	30	30½	31	31½	22	32½
1	4.7	4.9	5.1	5.3	5.4	5.6	5.8	6.0	6.3	6.5	6.7	6.9	7.1	7.3
2	9.4	9.8	10.1	10.5	10.9	11.3	11.7	12.1	12.5	12.9	13.3	13.8	14.2	14.7
3	14.1	14.6	15.2	14.8	16.3	16.9	17.5	18.1	18.8	19.4	20.0	20.7	21.3	22.0
4	18.8	19.5	20.3	21.0	21.8	22.6	23.4	24.2	25.0	25.8	26.7	27.6	28.4	29.3
5	23.5	24.4	25.3	26.3	27.2	28.2	29.2	30.2	31.3	32.3	33.4	34.5	35.6	36.7
6	28.2	29.3	30.4	31.5	32.7	33.8	35.0	36.3	37.5	38.8	40.0	41.3	42.7	44.0
7	32.9	34.1	35.4	36.8	38.1	39.4	40.9	42.3	43.8	45.2	46.7	48.2	49.8	51.3
8	37.6	39.0	40.5	42.0	43.6	45.1	46.7	48.3	50.0	51.7	53.4	55.1	56.9	58.7
9	42.3	43.9	45.6	47.3	49.0	50.8	52.6	54.4	56.3	58.1	60.1	62.0	64.0	66.0
0	46.9	48.8	50.6	52.5	54.4	56.4	58.4	60.4	62.5	64.6	66.7	68.9	71.1	73.4
1	51.6	53.6	55.7	57.8	59.9	62.0	64.2	66.5	68.8	71.1	73.4	75.8	78.2	80.7
2	56.3	58.5	60.8	63.0	65.3	67.7	70.1	72.5	75.0	77.5	80.1	82.7	85.3	88.0
3	61.0	63.4	65.8	68.3	70.8	73.3	75.9	78.6	81.3	84.0	86.8	89.6	92.4	95.4
4	65.7	68.3	70.9	73.5	76.2	79.0	81.8	84.6	87.5	90.4	93.4	96.5	99.6	102.7
5	70.4	73.2	75.9	78.8	81.7	84.6	87.6	90.7	93.8	96.9	100.1	103.4	106.7	110.0
6	75.1	78.0	81.0	84.0	87.1	90.3	93.4	96.7	100.0	103.4	106.8	110.3	113.8	117.4
7	79.8	82.9	86.1	89.3	92.6	95.9	99.3	102.7	106.3	109.8	113.5	117.1	120.9	124.7
8	84.5	87.8	91.1	94.5	98.0	101.5	105.1	108.8	112.5	116.3	120.1	124.0	128.0	132.0
9	89.2	92.7	96.2	99.8	103.4	107.2	111.0	114.8	118.8	122.7	125.8	130.9	135.1	139.4
0	93.9	97.5	101.3	105.0	103.9	112.8	116.8	120.9	125.0	129.2	133.5	137.8	142.2	146.7
1	98.6	102.4	106.3	110.3	114.3	118.5	122.6	125.9	131.3	135.7	140.1	144.7	149.3	154.0
2	103.3	107.3	111.4	115.5	119.8	124.1	128.5	133.0	137.5	142.1	146.8	151.6	156.4	161.4
3	108.0	112.2	116.4	120.8	125.2	129.7	134.3	139.0	143.8	148.6	153.5	158.5	163.6	168.7
4	112.7	117.0	121.5	125.0	130.7	135.4	140.2	145.0	150.0	155.0	160.2	165.4	170.7	175.0
5	117.4	121.9	126.6	131.3	136.1	141.0	146.0	151.1	156.3	161.5	166.8	172.3	177.8	183.4
6	122.1	126.8	131.6	136.5	141.6	145.7	151.8	157.1	162.5	168.0	173.5	179.2	184.9	190.7
7	126.8	131.7	136.7	141.8	147.0	152.3	157.7	163.2	168.8	174.4	180.2	186.0	192.0	198.0
8	131.4	136.5	141.8	147.0	152.4	157.9	163.5	169.2	175.0	180.9	186.9	192.9	199.1	205.4
9	136.1	141.4	145.8	152.3	157.9	163.6	169.4	175.3	181.3	187.3	193.5	199.8	206.2	212.7
0	140.8	146.3	151.9	157.6	163.3	169.2	175.2	181.3	187.5	193.8	200.2	206.7	213.3	220.1
1	145.5	151.2	156.9	162.8	163.8	174.9	181.0	187.3	193.8	200.3	206.9	213.6	220.4	227.4
2	150.2	156.1	162.0	168.1	174.2	180.5	186.9	193.4	200.0	206.7	213.6	220.5	227.6	234.7
3	154.9	160.9	167.1	173.3	179.7	185.1	192.7	199.4	206.3	213.2	220.2	227.4	234.7	242.1
4	159.6	165.8	172.1	178.6	185.1	191.8	198.6	205.5	212.5	219.6	226.9	234.3	241.8	249.4
5	164.3	170.7	177.2	183.8	190.6	197.4	204.4	211.5	218.8	226.1	233.6	241.2	248.9	256.7
6	169.0	175.6	182.3	189.1	195.0	203.1	210.3	217.5	225.0	232.6	240.3	248.1	255.0	254.1
7	173.7	180.4	187.3	194.3	201.4	208.7	216.1	223.6	231.3	239.0	246.9	255.0	263.1	271.4
8	178.4	185.3	192.4	199.6	206.9	214.3	221.9	229.6	237.5	245.5	253.6	261.8	270.2	278.7
9	183.1	190.2	197.4	204.8	212.3	220.0	227.8	235.7	243.8	251.7	260.3	258.7	277.3	286.1
0	187.8	195.1	202.5	210.1	217.8	225.6	233.6	241.7	250.0	258.4	266.5	275.6	284.4	293.4
41	192.5	199.9	207.6	215.3	223.2	231.3	239.5	247.8	256.3	264.9	273.6	282.5	291.6	300.7
42	197.2	204.8	212.6	220.6	228.7	236.9	245.3	253.8	262.5	271.3	280.3	289.4	298.7	308.1
43	201.9	209.7	217.7	225.8	234.1	242.5	251.1	257.0	268.8	277.8	287.0	296.3	305.8	315.4
44	205.6	214.6	222.8	231.1	239.6	248.2	257.0	265.9	275.0	284.2	293.6	303.2	312.9	322.7
45	211.3	219.5	227.8	235.3	245.0	253.8	262.8	272.0	281.3	290.7	300.3	310.1	320.0	330.1

Len. in Feet	The Fourth part of the Girt in Inches.													
	33	33½	34	34½	35	35½	36	36½	37	37½	38	38½	39	39½
1	7.6	7.8	8.0	8.3	8.5	8.8	9.0	9.3	9.5	9.8	10.0	10.3	10.6	10
2	15.1	15.6	16.1	16.5	17.0	17.5	18.0	18.5	19.0	19.5	20.1	20.6	21.1	2
3	22.7	23.4	24.1	24.8	25.5	26.3	27.0	27.8	28.5	29.3	30.1	30.9	31.7	3
4	30.3	31.2	32.1	33.1	34.0	35.0	36.0	37.0	38.0	39.1	40.1	41.2	42.3	4
5	37.8	39.0	40.1	41.3	42.5	43.8	45.0	46.3	47.5	48.8	50.1	51.5	52.8	5
6	45.4	46.8	48.2	49.6	51.0	52.5	54.0	55.5	57.0	58.6	60.2	61.8	63.4	6
7	52.9	54.6	56.2	57.9	59.5	61.3	63.0	64.8	66.5	68.4	70.2	72.1	73.9	7
8	60.5	62.3	64.2	66.1	68.1	70.0	72.0	74.0	76.1	78.1	80.2	82.3	84.5	8
9	68.1	70.1	72.3	74.4	76.6	78.8	81.0	83.3	85.6	87.9	90.3	92.6	95.1	9
10	75.6	77.9	80.3	82.7	85.1	87.5	90.0	92.5	95.1	97.7	100.3	102.9	105.6	10
11	83.2	85.7	88.3	90.9	93.6	96.3	99.0	101.8	104.6	107.4	110.3	113.2	116.2	11
12	90.8	93.5	96.3	99.2	102.1	105.0	108.0	111.0	114.1	117.2	120.3	123.5	126.8	13
13	98.3	101.3	104.4	107.5	110.6	113.8	117.0	120.3	123.6	127.0	130.4	133.8	137.3	14
14	105.9	109.1	112.4	115.7	119.1	122.5	126.0	129.5	133.1	136.7	140.4	144.1	147.9	15
15	113.4	116.9	120.4	124.0	127.6	131.3	135.0	138.8	142.6	146.5	150.4	154.4	158.4	16
16	121.0	124.7	128.4	132.3	136.1	140.0	144.0	148.0	152.1	156.3	160.4	164.7	169.0	17
17	128.6	132.5	136.5	140.5	144.6	148.8	153.0	157.3	161.6	166.0	170.5	175.0	179.6	18
18	136.1	140.3	144.5	148.8	153.1	157.5	162.0	166.5	171.1	175.8	180.5	185.3	190.1	19
19	143.7	148.1	152.5	157.0	161.6	166.3	171.0	175.8	180.6	185.5	190.5	195.6	200.7	20
20	151.3	155.9	160.6	165.3	170.1	175.0	180.0	185.0	190.1	195.3	200.6	205.9	211.3	21
21	158.8	163.7	168.6	173.6	178.6	183.8	189.0	194.3	199.6	205.1	210.6	216.2	221.8	22
22	166.4	171.5	176.6	181.8	187.2	192.5	198.0	203.5	209.2	214.8	220.6	225.5	232.4	23
23	173.9	179.2	184.6	190.1	195.7	201.3	207.0	212.8	218.7	224.6	230.6	236.7	242.9	24
24	181.5	187.0	192.7	198.4	204.2	210.0	216.0	222.0	228.2	234.4	240.7	247.0	253.5	26
25	189.1	194.8	200.7	206.6	212.7	218.8	225.0	231.3	237.7	244.1	250.7	257.3	264.1	27
26	196.6	202.6	208.7	214.9	221.2	227.5	234.0	240.5	247.2	253.9	260.7	267.6	274.6	28
27	204.2	210.4	216.8	223.2	229.7	236.3	243.0	249.8	256.7	263.7	270.8	277.9	285.2	29
28	211.8	218.2	224.8	231.4	238.2	245.0	252.0	259.0	266.2	273.4	280.8	288.2	295.8	30
29	219.3	226.0	232.8	239.7	246.7	253.8	261.0	268.3	275.7	283.2	290.8	298.5	306.3	31
30	226.9	233.8	240.8	248.0	255.2	262.6	270.0	277.6	285.2	293.0	300.8	308.8	316.9	32
31	234.4	241.6	248.9	256.2	263.7	271.3	279.0	286.8	294.7	302.7	310.9	319.1	327.4	33
32	242.0	249.4	256.9	264.5	272.2	280.1	288.0	296.1	304.2	312.5	320.9	329.4	338.0	34
33	249.6	257.2	264.9	272.8	280.7	288.8	297.0	305.3	313.7	322.3	330.9	339.7	348.6	35
34	257.1	265.0	272.9	281.0	289.2	297.6	306.0	314.6	323.2	332.0	340.9	350.0	359.1	36
35	264.7	272.8	281.0	289.3	297.7	306.3	315.0	323.8	332.7	341.8	351.0	360.3	369.7	37
36	272.3	280.6	289.0	297.6	306.3	315.1	324.0	333.1	342.3	351.6	361.0	370.6	380.3	39
37	279.8	288.4	297.0	305.8	314.8	323.8	333.0	342.3	351.8	361.3	371.0	380.9	390.8	40
38	287.4	296.1	305.1	314.1	323.3	332.6	342.0	351.6	361.3	371.1	381.1	391.1	401.4	41
39	294.9	303.9	313.1	322.4	331.8	341.3	351.0	360.8	370.8	380.9	391.1	401.4	411.9	42
40	302.5	311.7	321.1	330.6	340.3	350.1	360.0	370.1	380.3	390.6	401.1	411.7	422.5	43
41	310.1	319.5	329.1	338.9	348.8	358.8	369.0	379.3	389.8	400.4	411.1	422.0	433.1	44
42	317.6	327.3	337.2	347.2	357.3	367.6	378.0	388.6	399.3	410.2	421.2	432.3	443.6	45
43	325.2	335.1	345.2	355.4	365.8	376.3	387.0	397.8	408.8	419.9	431.2	442.6	454.2	46
44	332.8	342.9	353.2	363.7	373.3	385.1	396.0	407.1	418.3	429.7	441.2	452.9	464.8	47
45	340.3	350.7	361.3	372.0	381.8	393.8	405.0	416.3	427.8	439.5	451.3	463.2	475.3	48

The Fourth part of the Girt in Inches.													
40	40½	41	41½	42	42½	43	43½	44	44½	45	45½	46	46½
11.1	11.4	11.7	12.0	12.3	12.5	12.8	13.1	13.4	13.8	14.1	14.4	14.7	15.0
22.2	22.8	23.3	23.9	24.5	25.1	25.7	25.3	26.9	27.5	23.1	28.8	29.4	30.0
33.3	34.2	35.0	35.9	36.8	37.6	38.5	39.4	40.2	41.3	42.2	43.1	44.1	45.0
44.4	45.6	46.7	47.8	49.0	50.2	51.4	52.6	53.8	55.0	56.3	57.5	58.8	60.2
55.6	57.0	58.4	59.8	61.3	62.7	64.2	65.7	67.2	68.8	70.3	71.9	73.5	75.1
66.7	68.3	70.0	71.8	73.5	75.3	77.0	78.8	80.7	82.5	84.4	86.3	88.2	90.1
77.8	79.7	81.7	83.7	85.8	87.8	89.9	91.9	94.1	96.3	98.4	100.6	102.9	105.1
88.9	91.2	93.4	95.7	98.0	100.3	102.7	105.1	107.6	110.0	112.5	115.0	117.5	120.1
100.0	102.6	105.1	107.6	110.3	112.9	115.6	118.3	121.0	123.8	126.6	129.4	132.3	135.1
111.1	113.9	115.7	119.6	122.5	125.4	128.4	131.4	134.4	137.5	140.5	143.8	146.9	150.2
122.2	125.3	128.4	131.6	134.8	138.0	141.2	144.5	147.9	151.3	154.7	158.1	161.6	165.2
133.3	136.7	140.1	143.5	147.0	150.5	154.1	157.7	161.3	165.0	168.8	172.5	175.3	180.2
144.4	148.1	151.8	155.5	159.3	163.1	165.9	170.8	174.8	178.8	182.8	186.9	191.0	195.2
155.6	159.5	163.4	157.4	171.5	175.5	179.8	184.0	188.2	192.5	195.9	201.3	205.7	213.2
166.7	170.9	175.1	179.4	183.8	188.2	192.6	197.1	201.7	206.3	210.9	215.7	220.4	225.2
177.8	182.3	186.8	191.4	196.0	200.7	205.4	210.3	215.1	220.0	225.0	230.0	235.1	240.3
188.9	193.6	198.5	203.3	208.3	213.2	218.3	223.4	228.6	233.8	239.1	244.4	249.8	255.3
200.0	205.0	210.1	215.3	220.5	225.8	231.1	236.5	242.0	247.5	253.1	258.8	264.5	270.3
211.1	216.4	221.8	227.2	232.8	238.3	244.0	249.7	255.4	261.3	267.2	273.2	279.2	285.3
222.2	227.8	233.5	239.2	245.0	250.9	256.8	262.8	258.9	275.0	281.3	287.5	293.9	300.3
233.3	239.2	245.1	251.2	257.3	263.4	259.6	276.0	282.3	283.8	295.3	301.9	308.6	315.3
244.4	250.6	256.8	263.1	259.5	276.0	282.5	289.1	295.8	302.5	309.4	315.3	323.3	330.3
255.6	262.0	258.8	275.1	281.8	288.5	295.3	302.2	309.2	316.3	323.4	330.7	338.0	345.4
266.7	273.4	280.2	287.0	294.0	301.0	308.2	315.4	322.7	330.0	337.5	345.0	352.7	360.4
277.8	284.8	291.8	299.0	306.3	313.6	321.0	323.5	336.1	343.8	351.6	359.4	367.4	375.4
288.9	296.2	303.5	311.0	318.5	326.1	333.8	341.7	349.5	357.5	365.6	373.4	382.1	390.4
300.0	307.5	315.2	322.9	330.8	338.7	346.7	354.8	362.0	371.3	379.7	388.2	396.8	405.4
311.1	318.9	326.9	334.9	343.0	351.2	359.5	357.9	376.4	385.0	393.8	402.5	411.4	420.4
322.2	330.3	338.5	346.8	355.3	363.8	372.4	381.1	389.9	398.8	407.8	416.9	425.1	435.5
333.3	341.7	350.2	358.8	367.5	375.3	385.2	394.2	403.3	412.5	421.9	431.3	440.8	450.5
344.4	353.1	361.9	370.8	379.8	388.8	398.0	407.4	415.8	425.3	435.9	445.7	455.5	455.5
355.6	364.5	373.6	382.7	392.0	401.4	410.9	420.5	430.2	440.1	450.0	460.1	470.2	480.5
366.7	375.9	385.2	394.7	404.3	413.9	423.7	433.6	443.7	453.8	454.1	474.4	484.9	495.5
377.8	387.3	395.9	405.6	416.5	426.5	436.6	446.8	457.1	467.6	478.1	488.8	499.6	510.5
288.9	398.7	408.6	418.6	428.8	430.0	449.4	459.9	470.6	481.3	492.2	503.2	514.3	525.5
400.0	410.1	420.3	430.6	441.0	451.6	452.3	473.1	484.0	495.1	506.3	517.6	529.0	540.6
411.1	421.5	431.9	442.5	453.3	464.1	475.1	486.2	497.4	508.8	520.3	541.9	543.7	555.6
422.2	432.8	443.6	454.5	455.5	476.6	487.7	499.3	510.9	522.5	534.4	546.3	558.4	572.6
433.3	444.2	455.3	466.4	477.8	489.2	500.8	512.5	524.3	536.3	548.5	560.7	573.1	585.6
444.4	455.6	466.9	478.4	490.0	501.7	513.6	525.6	537.8	550.1	562.5	575.1	587.8	600.6
455.6	467.0	478.6	490.4	502.3	514.3	525.5	538.8	551.2	563.8	576.6	589.4	602.5	615.6
466.7	478.4	490.3	502.3	514.5	526.3	539.1	551.9	554.7	577.6	590.6	603.8	617.2	630.7
477.8	489.8	502.0	514.3	526.8	539.1	552.1	565.0	578.1	591.3	604.7	618.2	631.9	645.7
488.9	501.2	513.6	526.2	539.0	551.9	565.0	578.2	591.6	605.1	618.8	632.6	646.5	650.7
500.0	512.6	525.3	538.2	551.3	564.5	577.8	591.3	605.0	618.8	632.8	647.0	651.3	675.7

Y y   The

Len. in Feet	The Fourth part of the Girt in Inches.													
	47	47½	48	48½	49	49½	50	50½	51	51½	52	52½	53	53½
1	15.3	15.7	16.0	16.3	16.7	17.0	17.4	17.7	18.1	18.4	18.8	19.1	19.5	19.9
2	30.7	31.3	32.0	32.7	33.3	34.0	34.7	35.4	36.1	36.8	37.6	38.3	39.0	39.8
3	46.0	47.0	48.0	49.0	50.0	51.0	52.1	53.1	54.2	55.3	56.3	57.4	58.5	59.6
4	61.4	62.7	64.0	65.3	66.7	68.1	69.4	70.8	72.3	73.7	75.1	76.6	78.0	79.5
5	76.7	78.3	80.0	81.7	83.3	85.1	86.8	88.6	90.3	92.1	93.9	95.7	97.5	99.4
6	92.0	94.0	96.0	98.0	100.0	102.1	104.2	106.3	108.4	110.5	112.7	114.8	117.0	119.3
7	107.4	109.7	112.0	114.3	116.7	119.1	121.5	124.0	126.4	128.9	131.4	134.0	136.5	139.1
8	122.7	125.3	128.0	130.7	133.3	136.1	138.9	141.7	144.5	147.3	150.2	153.1	156.1	159.0
9	138.1	141.0	144.0	147.0	150.1	153.1	156.3	159.4	162.6	165.8	169.0	172.3	175.6	178.9
10	153.4	156.7	160.0	163.4	166.7	170.2	173.6	177.1	180.6	184.2	187.8	191.4	195.1	198.8
11	168.7	172.4	176.0	179.7	183.4	187.2	191.0	194.8	198.7	202.6	206.6	210.5	214.6	218.6
12	184.1	188.0	192.0	196.0	200.1	204.2	208.3	212.5	216.8	221.0	225.3	229.7	234.1	238.5
13	199.4	203.7	208.0	212.4	216.8	221.2	225.7	230.2	234.8	239.4	244.1	248.8	253.6	258.4
14	214.8	219.4	224.0	228.7	233.4	238.2	243.1	247.9	252.9	257.9	262.9	268.0	273.1	278.3
15	230.1	235.0	240.0	245.0	250.1	255.2	260.4	265.7	270.9	276.3	281.7	287.1	292.6	298.2
16	245.4	250.7	256.0	261.4	266.8	272.3	277.8	283.4	289.0	294.7	300.4	306.3	312.1	318.0
17	260.8	266.4	272.0	277.7	283.5	289.3	295.1	301.1	307.1	313.1	319.2	325.4	331.6	337.9
18	276.1	282.0	288.0	294.0	300.1	306.3	312.5	318.8	325.1	331.5	338.0	344.5	351.1	357.8
19	291.5	297.7	304.0	310.4	316.8	323.3	329.9	336.5	343.2	349.9	356.8	363.7	370.6	377.7
20	306.8	313.4	320.0	326.7	333.5	340.3	347.2	354.2	361.3	368.4	375.6	382.8	390.1	397.5
21	322.1	329.0	336.0	343.0	350.1	357.3	364.6	371.9	379.3	386.8	394.3	402.0	409.6	417.4
22	337.5	344.7	352.0	359.4	366.8	374.3	381.9	389.6	397.4	405.2	413.1	421.1	429.2	437.3
23	352.8	360.4	368.0	375.7	383.5	391.4	399.3	407.3	415.4	423.6	431.9	440.2	448.7	457.2
24	368.2	376.0	384.0	392.0	400.2	408.4	416.7	425.0	433.5	442.0	450.7	459.4	468.2	477.0
25	383.5	391.7	400.0	408.4	416.8	425.4	434.0	442.8	451.6	460.5	469.4	478.5	487.7	496.9
26	398.8	407.4	416.0	424.7	433.5	442.4	451.4	460.5	469.6	478.9	488.2	497.7	507.2	516.8
27	414.2	423.0	432.0	441.0	450.2	459.4	468.8	478.2	487.7	497.3	507.0	516.8	526.7	536.7
28	429.5	438.7	448.0	457.4	466.9	476.4	486.1	495.9	505.8	515.7	525.8	535.9	546.2	556.5
29	444.9	454.4	464.0	473.7	483.5	493.5	503.5	513.6	523.8	534.1	544.6	555.1	565.7	576.4
30	460.2	470.1	480.0	490.1	500.2	510.5	520.8	531.3	541.9	552.6	563.3	574.2	585.2	596.3
31	475.5	485.7	496.0	506.4	516.9	527.5	538.2	549.0	559.9	571.0	582.1	593.4	604.7	616.2
32	490.9	501.4	512.0	522.7	533.6	544.5	555.6	566.7	578.0	589.4	600.9	612.5	624.2	636.1
33	506.2	517.1	528.0	539.1	550.2	561.5	572.9	584.4	596.1	607.8	619.7	631.6	643.7	655.9
34	521.6	532.7	544.0	555.4	566.9	578.5	590.3	602.1	614.1	626.2	638.4	650.8	663.2	675.8
35	536.9	548.4	560.0	571.7	583.5	595.5	607.6	619.9	632.2	644.6	657.2	669.9	682.7	695.7
36	552.3	564.1	576.0	588.1	600.3	612.6	625.0	637.6	650.3	663.1	676.0	689.1	702.3	715.6
37	567.6	579.7	592.0	604.4	616.9	629.6	642.4	655.8	668.3	681.5	694.8	708.2	721.8	735.4
38	582.9	595.4	608.0	620.7	633.6	646.6	659.7	673.0	686.4	699.9	713.6	727.3	741.3	755.3
39	598.3	611.1	624.0	637.1	650.3	663.6	677.1	690.7	704.4	718.3	732.3	746.5	760.8	775.2
40	613.6	626.7	640.0	653.4	666.9	680.6	694.4	708.4	722.5	736.7	751.1	765.6	780.3	795.1
41	629.0	642.4	655.0	669.7	683.6	697.6	711.8	726.1	740.6	755.2	769.9	784.8	799.8	814.9
42	644.3	658.1	672.0	686.1	700.3	714.7	729.2	743.8	758.6	773.6	788.7	803.9	819.3	834.8
43	659.6	673.7	688.0	702.4	717.0	731.7	746.5	761.5	776.7	792.0	807.4	823.0	838.8	854.7
44	675.0	689.4	704.0	718.7	733.6	748.7	763.9	779.2	794.8	810.4	826.2	842.2	858.3	874.6
45	690.3	705.1	720.0	735.1	750.3	765.7	781.3	797.0	812.8	828.8	845.0	861.3	877.8	894.5

The Fourth part of the Girt in Inches.

54	54½	55	55½	56	56½	57	57½	58	58½	59	59½	60	60½
20.3	20.6	21.0	21.4	21.8	22.2	22.6	23.0	23.4	23.8	24.2	24.6	25.0	25.4
40.5	41.3	42.0	42.8	43.6	44.3	45.1	45.9	46.7	47.5	48.3	49.2	50.0	50.8
60.8	61.9	63.0	64.2	65.3	66.5	67.7	68.9	70.1	71.3	72.5	73.8	75.0	76.3
81.0	82.5	84.0	85.6	87.1	88.7	90.3	91.8	93.4	95.1	96.7	98.3	100.0	101.7
101.3	103.1	105.0	107.0	108.9	110.8	112.8	114.8	116.8	118.8	120.9	122.9	125.0	127.1
121.5	123.3	126.0	128.3	130.7	133.0	135.4	137.8	140.2	142.6	145.0	147.5	150.0	152.5
141.8	144.4	147.0	149.7	152.4	155.2	157.9	160.7	163.5	166.4	169.2	172.1	175.0	177.9
162.0	165.0	168.	171.1	174.2	177.3	180.5	183.7	186.9	190.1	193.4	196.7	200.0	203.3
182.3	185.6	189.1	192.5	196.0	199.5	203.1	206.6	210.3	213.9	217.6	221.3	225.0	228.8
202.5	206.3	210.1	213.9	217.8	221.7	225.6	229.6	233.6	237.7	241.7	245.9	250.0	254.2
222.8	226.9	231.1	235.3	239.6	243.9	248.2	252.6	257.0	261.4	265.9	270.4	275.0	279.6
243.0	247.5	252.1	256.7	261.3	266.0	270.8	275.5	280.3	285.2	290.1	295.0	300.0	305.0
263.3	268.1	273.1	278.1	283.1	288.2	293.3	298.5	303.7	309.0	314.3	319.6	325.0	330.4
283.5	288.8	294.1	299.5	304.9	310.4	315.9	321.4	327.1	332.7	338.4	344.2	350.0	355.9
303.8	309.4	315.1	320.9	326.7	332.5	338.4	344.4	350.4	356.5	362.6	368.8	375.0	381.3
324.0	330.0	336.1	342.3	348.4	354.7	361.0	367.4	373.8	380.3	386.8	393.4	400.0	406.7
344.3	350.7	357.1	363.6	370.2	376.9	383.6	390.3	397.1	404.0	411.0	417.9	425.0	432.1
364.5	371.3	378.1	385.0	392.0	399.0	406.1	413.3	420.5	427.8	435.1	442.5	450.0	457.5
384.8	391.9	399.1	406.4	413.8	421.2	428.7	436.2	443.9	451.5	459.3	467.1	475.0	482.9
405.0	412.5	420.1	427.8	435.6	443.4	451.3	459.2	467.2	475.2	483.5	491.7	500.0	508.4
425.3	433.2	441.1	449.2	457.3	465.5	473.8	482.1	490.6	499.1	507.6	516.3	525.0	533.8
445.5	453.8	462.2	470.6	479.1	487.7	496.4	505.1	513.9	522.8	531.8	540.9	550.0	559.2
465.8	474.4	483.2	492.0	500.9	509.9	518.9	528.1	537.3	546.6	556.0	565.5	575.0	584.6
486.0	495.0	504.2	513.4	522.7	532.0	541.5	551.0	560.7	570.4	580.2	590.0	600.0	610.0
506.3	515.7	525.2	534.8	544.4	554.2	564.1	574.0	584.0	594.1	604.3	614.6	625.0	635.5
526.5	536.3	546.2	556.2	566.2	576.4	586.6	597.0	607.4	617.9	628.5	639.2	650.0	660.9
546.8	556.9	567.2	577.5	583.0	598.5	609.2	619.9	630.8	641.7	652.7	663.8	675.0	686.3
567.0	577.5	588.2	598.9	609.8	620.7	631.8	642.9	654.1	665.4	676.9	688.4	700.0	711.7
587.3	598.2	609.2	620.3	631.6	642.9	654.3	665.8	677.5	689.2	701.0	713.0	725.0	737.1
607.5	618.8	630.2	641.7	653.3	665.1	676.9	688.8	700.8	713.0	725.2	737.6	750.0	762.6
627.8	639.4	651.2	663.1	675.1	687.2	699.4	711.8	724.2	736.7	749.4	762.1	775.0	788.0
648.0	660.1	672.2	684.5	696.9	709.4	722.0	734.7	747.6	760.5	773.6	786.7	800.0	813.4
668.3	680.7	693.2	705.9	718.7	731.6	744.6	757.7	770.9	784.3	797.7	811.3	825.0	838.8
688.5	701.3	714.2	727.3	740.4	753.7	767.1	780.6	794.3	808.0	821.9	835.9	850.0	864.2
708.8	721.9	735.2	748.7	762.2	775.9	789.7	803.6	817.6	831.8	846.1	860.5	875.0	889.6
729.0	742.6	756.3	770.1	784.0	798.1	812.3	826.6	841.0	855.5	870.3	885.1	900.0	915.1
749.3	763.2	777.3	791.3	805.8	820.2	834.8	849.5	864.4	879.3	894.4	909.6	925.0	940.5
769.5	783.8	798.3	812.8	827.6	842.4	857.4	872.5	887.7	903.1	918.6	934.3	950.0	965.9
789.8	804.4	819.3	834.2	849.3	864.6	879.9	895.4	911.1	926.9	942.8	958.8	975.0	991.3
810.0	825.1	840.3	855.6	871.1	886.7	902.5	918.4	934.4	950.6	966.9	983.4	1000.0	1016.7
830.3	845.7	861.3	877.0	892.9	908.9	925.1	941.4	957.8	974.4	991.1	1008.0	1025.0	1042.2
850.5	866.3	882.3	898.4	914.7	931.1	947.6	964.3	981.2	998.2	1015.3	1032.6	1050.0	1067.6
870.8	886.9	903.3	919.8	936.4	953.2	970.2	987.3	1004.5	1021.9	1039.5	1057.2	1075.0	1093.0
891.0	907.6	924.3	941.2	958.2	975.4	992.8	1010.2	1027.9	1045.8	1063.6	1081.7	1100.0	1118.4
911.3	928.2	945.3	962.6	980.0	997.6	1015.3	1033.2	1051.3	1069.5	1087.8	1106.3	1135.0	1143.8

Len. in Feet	61	61½	62	62½	63	63½	64	64½	65	65½	66	66½	67	67
					The Fourth part of the Girt in Inches.									
1	25.8	26.3	20.7	27.1	27.6	28.0	28.4	28.9	29.3	29.8	30.3	30.7	31.2	3
2	51.7	52.5	53.4	54.3	55.1	56.2	56.9	57.8	58.7	59.6	60.5	61.4	02.3	63
3	77.5	78.8	80.1	81.4	82.7	84.0	85.3	86.7	88.0	89.4	90.8	92.1	93.5	9
4	103.4	105.1	106.8	108.5	110.3	112.0	113.8	115.6	117.4	119.2	121.0	122.8	124.7	126
5	129.2	131.3	133.5	135.6	137.8	140.0	142.2	144.5	146.7	149.0	151.3	153.6	155.9	158
6	155.0	157.6	160.2	162.8	165.4	168.0	170.7	173.3	176.0	178.8	181.5	184.3	187.0	189
7	180.9	183.9	186.9	189.9	192.9	196.0	199.1	202.2	205.4	208.6	211.8	215.0	218.2	221
8	206.7	210.1	213.6	217.0	220.5	224.0	227.6	231.1	234.7	238.3	242.0	245.7	249.4	253
9	232.6	236.4	240.3	244.1	248.1	252.0	256.0	260.0	264.1	268.1	272.3	276.4	280.6	284
10	258.4	262.7	266.9	271.3	275.6	280.0	284.4	288.9	293.4	297.9	302.5	307.1	311.7	316
11	284.2	288.9	293.6	298.4	303.2	308.0	312.9	317.8	322.7	327.7	332.8	337.8	342.9	348
12	310.1	315.2	320.3	325.5	330.8	336.0	341.3	346.7	352.1	357.5	363.0	368.5	374.1	379
13	335.9	341.5	347.0	352.6	358.3	364.0	369.8	375.6	381.4	387.3	393.3	399.2	405.3	411
14	361.8	367.7	373.7	379.8	385.9	392.0	398.2	404.5	410.8	417.1	423.5	429.9	436.4	443
15	387.6	394.0	400.4	406.9	413.4	420.0	426.7	433.4	440.1	446.9	453.8	460.7	467.6	474
16	413.4	420.3	427.1	434.0	441.0	448.0	455.1	462.3	469.4	476.7	484.0	491.4	498.8	506
17	439.3	446.5	453.8	461.1	468.6	476.0	483.6	491.1	498.8	506.5	514.3	522.1	530.0	537
18	465.1	472.5	480.5	488.3	496.1	504.0	512.0	520.0	528.1	536.3	544.5	552.8	561.1	569
19	491.0	499.0	507.2	515.4	523.7	532.0	540.4	548.9	557.5	566.1	574.8	583.5	592.3	601
20	516.8	525.3	533.9	542.5	551.3	560.0	568.9	577.8	586.8	595.9	605.0	614.2	623.5	632
21	542.6	551.6	560.6	569.7	578.8	588.0	597.3	605.7	616.1	625.7	635.3	644.9	654.6	664
22	568.5	577.8	587.3	596.8	606.4	616.0	625.8	635.6	645.5	655.5	665.5	675.6	685.8	696
23	594.3	604.1	614.0	623.9	633.5	644.0	654.2	664.5	674.8	685.2	695.8	706.3	717.0	727
24	620.2	630.4	640.7	651.0	661.5	672.0	682.7	693.4	704.1	715.0	726.0	737.0	748.2	759
25	646.0	656.6	667.4	678.2	689.1	700.0	711.1	722.3	733.5	744.8	756.3	767.8	779.3	791
26	671.8	682.9	694.1	705.3	716.6	728.0	739.6	751.2	762.8	774.6	785.5	798.5	810.5	822
27	697.7	709.2	720.8	732.4	744.2	756.0	768.0	780.0	792.2	804.4	816.8	829.2	841.7	854
28	723.5	735.4	747.4	759.5	771.8	784.0	795.4	808.9	821.5	834.2	847.0	859.9	872.9	885
29	749.4	761.7	774.1	786.7	799.3	812.1	824.9	837.8	850.9	864.0	877.3	890.6	904.0	917
30	775.2	788.0	800.8	813.8	826.5	840.0	853.3	866.7	880.2	893.8	907.5	921.3	935.2	949
31	801.0	814.2	827.5	840.5	854.4	868.1	881.8	895.6	909.5	923.6	937.8	952.0	966.4	980
32	826.9	842.5	854.2	868.1	882.0	896.1	910.2	924.5	938.9	953.4	968.0	982.7	997.6	1012
33	852.7	866.8	880.5	895.2	909.0	924.1	938.7	953.4	968.2	983.2	998.3	1013.4	1028.7	1044
34	878.6	893.0	907.0	922.3	937.1	952.1	967.1	982.3	997.6	1013.0	1028.5	1044.1	1059.9	1075
35	904.4	919.3	934.3	949.4	964.7	980.1	995.6	1011.2	1026.9	1042.8	1058.8	1074.9	1091.1	1107
36	930.3	945.6	961.0	976.6	992.3	1008.1	1024.0	1040.1	1056.3	1072.6	1089.0	1105.6	1122.3	1139
37	956.1	971.8	987.7	1003.7	1019.8	1036.1	1052.4	1069.0	1085.6	1102.4	1119.3	1136.3	1153.4	1170
38	981.9	998.1	1014.4	1030.8	1047.6	1064.1	1080.9	1097.8	1114.9	1132.1	1149.5	1167.0	1184.6	1202
39	1007.8	1024.4	1041.0	1057.5	1074.1	1092.1	1109.3	1126.7	1144.3	1161.9	1179.8	1197.7	1215.8	1234
40	1033.6	1050.6	1067.8	1085.1	1102.5	1120.1	1137.8	1155.6	1173.6	1191.7	1210.0	1228.4	1246.9	1265
41	1059.5	1076.9	1094.5	1112.2	1130.1	1148.1	1166.2	1184.5	1203.0	1221.5	1240.3	1259.1	1278.1	1297
42	1085.3	1103.2	1121.2	1139.3	1157.6	1176.1	1194.7	1213.4	1232.3	1251.3	1270.5	1289.8	1309.3	1328
43	1111.1	1129.4	1147.9	1166.4	1185.2	1204.1	1223.1	1242.3	1261.6	1281.1	1300.8	1320.5	1340.5	1360
44	1137.0	1155.7	1174.6	1193.6	1212.6	1232.1	1251.6	1271.2	1291.0	1310.9	1331.0	1351.2	1371.6	1392
45	1162.8	1182.0	1201.3	1220.7	1240.3	1260.1	1280.0	1300.1	1320.3	1340.7	1361.3	1382.0	1402.8	1423

The Fourth part of the Girt in Inches.

68	68½	69	69½	70	70½	71	71½	72	72½	73	73½	74	74½
32.1	32.6	33.1	33.5	34.0	34.5	35.0	35.5	36.0	36.5	37.0	37.5	38.0	38.5
64.2	65.2	66.1	67.1	68.1	69.0	70.0	71.0	72.0	73.0	74.0	75.0	76.1	77.1
96.3	97.8	99.2	100.6	102.1	103.5	105.0	106.5	108.0	109.5	111.0	112.5	114.1	115.6
128.4	130.3	132.3	134.2	136.1	138.1	140.0	142.0	144.0	146.0	148.0	150.1	152.1	154.2
160.6	162.9	165.3	167.7	170.1	172.6	175.0	177.5	180.0	182.5	185.0	187.6	190.1	192.7
192.7	195.5	198.4	201.3	204.2	207.1	210.0	213.0	216.0	219.0	222.0	225.1	228.2	231.3
224.8	228.1	231.4	234.8	238.2	241.6	245.0	248.5	252.0	255.5	259.0	262.6	266.2	269.8
256.9	260.7	264.5	268.3	272.2	276.1	280.0	284.0	288.0	292.0	296.1	300.1	304.2	308.3
289.0	293.3	297.6	301.9	306.3	310.6	315.1	319.5	324.0	328.5	333.1	337.6	342.3	346.9
321.1	325.9	330.6	335.4	340.3	345.2	350.1	355.0	360.0	365.0	370.1	375.2	380.3	385.4
353.2	358.4	363.7	369.0	374.3	379.7	385.1	390.5	395.0	401.5	407.1	412.7	418.3	424.0
385.3	391.0	396.8	402.5	408.3	414.2	420.1	426.0	432.0	438.0	444.1	450.2	456.3	462.5
417.4	423.6	429.8	436.1	442.4	448.7	455.1	461.5	468.0	474.5	481.1	487.7	494.4	501.1
449.6	456.2	462.9	469.6	476.4	483.2	490.1	497.0	504.0	511.0	518.1	525.2	532.4	539.6
481.7	488.8	495.9	503.2	510.4	517.7	525.1	532.5	540.0	547.5	555.1	562.7	570.4	578.2
513.8	521.4	529.0	536.7	544.4	552.3	560.1	568.0	576.0	584.0	592.1	600.3	608.4	616.7
545.9	553.9	562.1	570.2	578.5	586.8	595.1	603.5	612.0	620.5	629.1	637.8	646.5	655.2
578.0	586.5	595.4	603.8	612.5	621.3	630.1	639.0	648.0	657.0	666.1	675.3	684.5	693.8
610.1	619.1	628.2	637.3	646.5	655.8	665.1	674.5	684.0	693.5	703.1	712.8	722.5	732.3
642.2	651.7	661.3	670.9	680.6	690.3	700.1	710.0	720.0	730.0	740.1	750.3	760.6	770.9
674.3	684.3	694.3	704.4	714.6	724.8	735.1	745.0	756.0	766.5	777.1	787.8	798.6	809.4
706.4	716.9	727.4	738.0	748.6	759.3	770.2	781.0	792.0	803.0	814.2	825.3	836.6	848.0
738.6	749.5	760.4	771.5	782.6	793.9	805.2	816.5	828.0	839.5	851.2	862.9	874.6	886.5
770.7	782.0	793.5	805.0	816.7	828.4	840.2	852.0	864.0	876.0	888.2	900.4	912.7	925.0
802.8	814.6	826.6	838.6	850.7	862.9	875.2	887.5	900.0	912.5	925.2	937.9	950.7	963.6
834.9	847.2	859.6	872.1	884.7	897.4	910.2	923.0	936.0	949.0	962.2	975.4	988.7	1002.1
867.0	879.8	892.7	905.7	918.8	931.9	945.2	958.5	972.0	985.5	999.2	1012.9	1026.8	1040.7
899.1	912.4	925.8	939.2	952.8	966.4	980.2	994.0	1008.0	1022.0	1036.2	1050.4	1064.8	1079.2
931.2	945.0	958.9	972.8	986.8	1001.0	1015.2	1029.6	1044.0	1058.5	1073.2	1088.0	1102.8	1117.8
963.3	977.6	991.9	1006.3	1020.8	1035.5	1050.2	1065.1	1080.0	1095.1	1110.2	1125.5	1140.8	1156.3
995.4	1010.1	1024.9	1039.8	1054.9	1070.0	1085.2	1100.6	1116.0	1131.6	1147.2	1163.0	1178.9	1194.8
1027.6	1042.7	1058.0	1073.4	1088.9	1104.5	1120.2	1136.1	1152.0	1168.1	1184.2	1200.5	1216.9	1233.4
1059.7	1075.3	1091.1	1106.9	1122.9	1139.0	1155.2	1171.6	1188.0	1204.6	1221.2	1238.0	1254.9	1271.9
1091.8	1107.9	1124.1	1140.5	1156.9	1173.5	1190.2	1207.1	1224.0	1241.1	1258.2	1275.5	1292.9	1310.5
1123.9	1140.5	1157.2	1174.0	1191.0	1208.0	1225.2	1242.6	1260.0	1277.6	1295.2	1313.0	1331.0	1349.0
1156.0	1173.1	1190.3	1207.6	1225.0	1242.6	1260.3	1278.1	1296.0	1314.1	1332.3	1350.6	1369.0	1387.6
1188.1	1205.6	1223.3	1241.1	1259.0	1277.1	1295.3	1313.6	1332.0	1350.6	1369.3	1388.1	1407.0	1426.1
1220.2	1238.2	1256.4	1274.6	1293.1	1311.6	1330.3	1349.1	1368.0	1387.1	1406.3	1425.6	1445.1	1464.6
1252.3	1270.8	1289.4	1308.2	1327.1	1346.1	1365.3	1384.6	1404.0	1423.6	1443.3	1463.1	1483.1	1503.2
1284.4	1303.4	1322.5	1341.7	1361.1	1380.6	1400.3	1420.1	1440.0	1460.1	1480.3	1500.6	1521.1	1541.7
1316.6	1336.0	1355.6	1375.3	1395.1	1415.1	1435.4	1455.6	1476.0	1496.6	1517.3	1538.1	1559.1	1580.3
1348.7	1368.6	1388.6	1408.8	1429.2	1449.7	1470.3	1491.1	1512.0	1533.1	1554.3	1575.6	1597.2	1618.8
1380.8	1401.1	1421.7	1442.4	1463.2	1484.2	1505.3	1526.6	1548.0	1569.6	1591.3	1613.2	1635.2	1657.4
1412.9	1433.7	1454.8	1475.9	1497.2	1518.7	1540.3	1562.1	1584.0	1606.1	1623.3	1650.3	1673.2	1695.9
1445.0	1466.3	1487.8	1509.5	1531.3	1553.2	1575.3	1597.6	1620.0	1642.6	1665.3	1688.2	1711.3	1734.5

AN
APPENDIX,

SHEWING

The Way to Plenty:

Propos'd to the FARMERS;

Wherein are laid down

General Rules and Directions for the
Management and *Improvement* of a F A R M.

1 **WILD Oats** being one of the greatest Annoyances to the *Farmer*, no Care and Pains can be too much to destroy them. And altho' their Encrease be *chiefly* owing to a long continuance of *Plowing* and Tillage, yet the following Method pursued, (even in a regular course of Husbandry) is found the best and most effectual way to destroy them, *viz.*

After

After the *first* time of Summer-fallowing the Land, (in *March* or *April* suppose) in a month's time, and after a Showre, let the Harrow be drawn over the Fallow, and then you will quickly find the *wild Oats* to spring and appear : Let them continue to grow till the time of their *earing*, and with a Scyth mow 'em down, and in a dry Day, as soon after as may be, plow them all in ; which will be a means not only to mellow and *enrich* the Ground, but to kill and destroy that *pernicious Weed*, with the help of the after-turnings of the Land. 'Tis possible this first Experiment may not effectually and totally accomplish the destruction of this *Weed*, on the account of wet seasons, or some other accidental Causes, but it is known to be an *Excellent Remedy*, and therefore a resolute repetition of it will not fail to compleat the Cure. The only Objection to this method is, that the *Midsummer* Fallow is lost, and the Land will not have had sufficient tillage for *Wheat* at *Michaelmas :* But the Answer is, that it will do for *Barley* (which is not sown till Spring) by the help of an *Autumn* or *Winter*-fallowing ; and so the trial is to be made successively only on the Land intended for *Barley*.

II. **Instead** of *three* Fields for Tillage, (as the common practice is) *all* late Experience teacheth * **four** are better for the Farm and the Farmer, *viz.* (1) Wheat or Barley after the Fallows. (2) Pease or Beans, or rather *both*. (3) Oats; and then (4) the Summer Fallows. The reason of which is founded thus ; That a Crop of Beans and Pease do not (as

---

* In such places where the soil is a rich Loame, this course of Husbandry has answer'd to a wonder: But in others, where the soil is light, and not strong enough for Wheat and Beans, the common method of three Fields, or rather to take but one Crop, and then a Fallow, and so alternately, as is practis'd upon the light Lands in *Essex*, answers much the best.

most

moſt other grain) take *from,* but give Riches *to* the Land, *mellowing* and diſpoſing it for an After-crop : That the Straw of a mixt crop of Beans and Peaſe is a great Relief to Cattle in the winter, and excellently ſupplieth the want of Hay ; and, That a crop of Beans is as good, and ſometimes *better* than a crop of *Wheat.* Only becauſe it cannot be expected that the Land ſhould never be weary, and becauſe 'tis deſirable to *improve* poor Land as much as may be, therefore a ſmall quantity of ſuch Dung as can be got ſhould be laid upon the Bean-ſtubbles, as well as the uſual proportion upon the Fallows.

It ſhould alſo be here remember'd, that *Beans* and *Peaſe* (let the Soil be never ſo ſtrong) ſhould be ſown **Under-furrow**, *i. e. upon* the Stubbles, and plow'd *in* ; the Furrow to be *thin,* and laid *flat* upon the *Beans :* And this, if poſſible, ſhould be perform'd the latter end of *January,* or before the end of *February,* for no Froſt will hurt 'em after that : But as ſoon as they begin to *peep,* in *March,* and after a Showre, a Harrow ſhould be drawn over 'em (*fear not the tread of the Horſes*) to mellow and looſen the Earth, and make it fit to receive the fatning Dews. This method beſt ſecures the *Seed* from *Crows* and *Pigeons,* and at the ſame time gives a proper *depth of Earth* as a defence and ſecurity againſt the Droughts at *Midſummer,* when they are in bloſſom, and when (for want of it) they are apt to ſhrink and *wither away.*

III. **When Land** is over-run with Shrubs, Underwood, Whins, Brakes, and by Age becomes *moſſy,* and for want of trenching is poachy and full of Boggs, the firſt and only Remedy is, to clear the Ground of all the Trumpery, and then to *ſet in* the Plough for three years, ſowing only *Oats* thereon ſucceſſively, except it be good and proper enough to ſow *Barley* the third year ; ſtill always remembring to keep

a ſufa fufficient number of Trenches open to drain the Land ; and with the third and laft Crop to fow *Grafs-feeds* ✳ fuited to the nature of the Soil, fuch as *Clover, Trefoil, Rye-grafs,* &c. with a view to continue it in Pafture for three or four years, and then to *fet in* the Plough again ; and, if the Land is not of the beft fort, to continue it fo fucceffively.   But it fhould not be forgot, that before every third Crop is fown, a convenient quantity of *Coal-afhes,* if poffible, or fuch other Manure as the place will afford, fhould be laid on, the better to make it fward over ; ten wain-loads on an Acre will do pretty well.

IV. **Altho**' it be needlefs to fay, that all Dungs are Improvers of Land, both Pafture and Tillage, fuch as the Dung of Horfes, Cows, Sheep, Hogs ; as alfo *Fifh,* † *Sea-fand* and *Shells, Rags, Leather, Tanners-Bark, Kilp-afhes,* &c. yet becaufe it is not throughly underftood, and therefore too oft neglected, a ftrefs is to be laid upon the peculiar Excellency and Goodnefs of *Coal-Afhes,* (but efpecially the [a] Afhes of Sea-Coal burnt) for all Pafture and Meadow

---

✳ See the Particulars at the end of this Appendix.

† The great Neglect of the Tenants along the Northern Coafts, in not laying *Sea-Sand* upon their Tillage, which chiefly confifts of a ftiff Clay, and would (of all other Soils) be moft *Improv'd* by it.

[a] I was not a little *furpriz'd* when I firft went down to furvey and let *His Grace the Duke of* BUCKINGHAM's *Eftates in Yorkfhire,* to find the Tenants had fuffer'd *Millions* of Loads of Sea-coal-afhes (made from the vaft quantities of Coal ufed in the *Allom*-works at *Sandfend*) to be wafh'd into the Sea for above 100 years laft paft, without ever laying them upon their Pafture and Meadow Grounds   Had the Tenants known the Vertue of thefe Coal-afhes from the beginning of the *Allom*-works, the Eftate might have been confiderably *Improv'd* ; but fince, care has been taken to oblige all the Tenants to follow the Example of the Tenants round *Sunderland* and *Newcaftle,* who have made great *Improvements* very lately by vertue of this Noble Manure of Sea-coal-afhes.

Ground,

Ground, provided they be well freed from the Cynders; the nature and vertue whereof is such, that it immediately disposeth the Land to produce wild *Trefoil*, and all the best and sweetest Grasses, and in such abundance also, that it will soon keep a double number of Stock, and produce double the Loads of Hay. As was said before, ten Loads on an Acre will do, but more is better, where it can easily be had.

V. **Experience** hath shewn, that even the worst Land may be so order'd that it shall in some measure *improve it self*, without any **Super=inductions** or Dung. *Turnips* for instance (which are too much neglected in the *North*) sown at *Midsummer*, and kept regularly * *houghed*, will not only *support*, but † *fatten* Sheep in the Winter in great numbers, and consequently *enrich* the Soil by their *Dung* and *Urine*. And the very *Refuse* of the Turnips, after the Sheep have scoop'd 'em, and are become rotten, do strangely mellow and fatten the Soil, richly disposing it for a crop of *Oats*, *Barley*, or *Spring-Wheat*, without any *Super-induction* of Dung. But in this process it is to be remember'd, that the Sheep are to be confined to *one Acre* at a time, by proper Hurdles, not suffering them to *ramble* over the *whole* at once.

Again, **Clover** sown on indifferent Land, or Land *worn* out with plowing, if at *Midsummer* (when 'tis in its full blos-

---

* See the Method of houghing Turnips in the following pages, where 'tis fully describ'd.

† When Sheep are made fat with Turnips, 'tis adviseable to turn 'em into a Pasture for about a fortnight before they are kill'd, (especially if they are to be drove) by which means the nicest Palate cannot discover the taste of Turnip-fed Mutton from the finest Grass Mutton.

fom and pride) it be plow'd in, will quickly fink and die away, and by its Salts give an uncommon fertility to the Soil, mellowing and *enriching* it for two or three Crops fuc-ceffively, beginning with a Crop of *Wheat* in *Autumn*, after another Fallow.   Much the fame (tho' not in fo good a degree) is to be faid with refpect to *Peafe*, *Vetches*, *Lentils*, and *Buck-wheat*.   However, it fhould not be *diffembled* that the hazard of fowing Turnips on *very poor* Land is great, without fome additional help ; and therefore a fprinkling of any rotten Dung, Hen or Pigeon-dung, Malt-duft, Coal or Kilp or Turf-afhes, may be proper to be thrown on before the Sowing at *Midfummer* or *Lammas*, after the Ground is made fine with the Bufh-Harrow.

VI. **Clover, Trefoil, Saintfoin, Rye=grafs,** &c. (of which fee more in this Appendix) are vaft Improve-ments to Lands, efpecially the worft fort, and thofe that are defign'd to be laid down for Pafture, and after a reafonable time to be plow'd up again, by bringing them fuddenly to Turf, and by the richnefs of the Feed, caufing them to keep near three times the number of Cattle which otherwife they could do.   But there is a Caution here to be obferv'd, efpe-cially with refpect to large Cattle, *viz.* that for the *firft week* when they are turn'd into it, you do not fuffer them to con-tinue in it above an *Hour* at a time, (an *Hour* at each Noon is fufficient) for otherwife they will be apt to furfeit, to fwell and die.   But the Improvement here fpoken of, manag'd with difcretion, is furprizing to them who have not feen it, and is one of the late means whereby Farmers have gain'd great Riches to themfelves.   Thus the known Maxim here takes place, That *an Encreafe of the Stock is always a double En-creafe of the Profit* ; return'd to the Farmer thefe two ways,
                                                                        both

both in the Profit of fat Cattle, and in the *Improvement* of his Land for another Year.

VII. 𝔄𝔩𝔱𝔥𝔬' the nature of Seed-Corn, and the time of sowing it, is thought to be pretty well underſtood, yet there are great miſtakes often committed by Farmers (of the *North* eſpecially) in this affair. All Winter-corn ſhould be ſown rather *before* than *after Michaelmas*, eſpecially *Rye* on the ligh-teſt Land; and therefore the *firſt* fair and ſettled weather that offers after *September* ſets in, ſhould be choſen, and the *Fallows* ſhou'd be diſpos'd and prepar'd accordingly: Not but that, if the Seaſon ſuit not in *September*, or even *October*, he may with a great deal of reaſon hope for Succeſs any time in *November*, and ſometimes later; but yet, I repeat it again, if Choice may be had, at or before *Michaelmas* is beſt for moſt Land, eſpecially in the *North*. In the management of his *Fallows*, the Farmer ſhould on no account go out with his Team in a *wet* Day, ſuch practice conſtantly tending to *ſett* the weeds, and to make the Land lie *foul* at Seed-time.

𝔅𝔦𝔤 is a Grain known only in the *North*, and deſerves to be *baniſh'd* thence; for the Drink made of it is very diſagree-able to Strangers, and affords not a proportionable Strength equal to the ſame quantity of *Barley*, which yet always ex-ceeds it in price about two-pence in the Buſhel. 'Tis alſo a miſtake to think it will grow and thrive where *Barley* will not; for it requires both the *ſame Management* and the *ſame Soil*: Neither will it afford a *greater Encreaſe*; for tho' it hath a ſquare Ear, and *four rows* of Corn, yet that advantage is more than counterbalanc'd by the *Leanneſs* of the Grain, and the *Thickneſs* of the Skin.

B b b

𝔅𝔞𝔯=

Barley is a hardier Grain than is commonly imagin'd, and therefore fhould be fown (if poffible) in *February*, the fucceeding Frofts never hurting it. The common and ufual way is, to harrow it in after plowing; which doth well enough with early fowing, or a wet Spring : But late Experience fhews, that except the Land be very ftrong indeed, fowing it **Under=furrow** (like Beans) is the fureft way with all accidents to obtain a *great* Encreafe. Some take the middle way, fowing half *under*, and half *above* furrow, and have fucceeded very well. A very light Soil, that runs much to *Weeds*, is an Exception to an early fowing, but not to a late one **under=furrow.** Great Care ought to be taken to weed both *Wheat* and *Barley* in *May* and *June*, for Experience fheweth that the higheft Expence in doing it is always repaid. *Carlock* is an harmlefs *Weed*, but no Grain fuffers fo much as *Wheat* and *Barley* by *Thiftles*, *Docks*, &c. If after weeding the Crop appears thin, 'tis very advifeable to ftrew Pigeon or Hen-dung, or Kilp-afhes, or Malt-duft over it, by which means it will ftrangely encreafe and *gather*; but this work is moft proper to be done in rainy weather.

VIII. **Becaufe Lime** is found by all late Experience to be an excellent *Improver* of Tillage-Land, the Ufe of it is ftrongly recommended, where-ever it can be had at any tolerable rate. It agrees with all forts of Soils, except the two Extreams, of a dufty *blowing Sand*, and the *ftrongeft Clays :* Where there is any good degree of the mixture of *both*, it never faileth to make *vaft Improvements*; for by its holding nature, when throughly dead and fallen, it adds *Tenacity* to light Soils, thereby hind'ring the Rains from falling too foon away ; and, by its Salts, opens and relaxes
the

the ftronger Soils, that they are not chill'd and ftarv'd by *ftagnating* wets : For which reafon all *Heaths,* and *Moors* and Grounds over-run with *Whins, Brakes, Broom,* or other brufhy Underwood, when turn'd up with the Plough, are furprizingly benefited by it ; infomuch that many Lands, fuppos'd before to be not worth above Two fhillings an Acre, are in the *North of* ENGLAND made to be worth Twenty fhillings an Acre, by vertue of this noble Manure of **Lime,** Eighty or Ninety Bufhels whereof being laid on an *Acre* in Tillage, will laft Four or Five Years. But it fhould always be remember'd, that all loofe, heathy, or moorifh light Soils, after fowing for three or four years, or fo long as the Soil continues hollow or fpongy, fhould (as foon as the Spring-Corn begins to appear) be *rolled* with a long *heavy* wooden *Roll,* the better to faften the Ground, and to *clofe* the Corn to it ; which Practice is not yet underftood in all parts of the *North,* and there-fore their Crops often fail in a dry Summer for want of it : Or they *weakly* content themfelves to lofe the firft year's Crop, and fo are at the charge of two or three *Fal-lows,* only to obtain an End which is much better obtain'd by ROLLING.

IX. **In laying down** the Land after tillage (always fuppos'd to have been done with fowing **Clover,** &c.) great care fhould be taken that the Ridges be not laid *too high,* which always proves a damage to either Pafture or Meadow ; for in *high* Ridges the good Soil is thrown up *deeper than neceffary* at the *top,* and the Furrows laid bare to the *hungry bottom,* which bears nothing but coarfe Grafs or Rufhes. But yet it fhould ever be remember'd, that pro-per Drains fhould be made from the *higheft* to the *loweft*
places,

places, that the Water may not *ftagnate* any where, but be carried into the Water-courfes: For tho' a due quantity of moifture be neceffary for vegetation, yet Water (where-ever there is *too much*, fo as to *ftagnate*) always *impoverifhes* the Land: And therefore, in this *neceffary Work* of *drain-ing*, let the Trench open'd be conveniently *wide* and *deep* enough; and what is taken out with the Spade fhould not be laid too near the fide of the Drain, left it be poach'd in again by the Feet of the Cattle.

X. **Great Improvements** are made in many parts of *Effex*, by laying on their Land the Earth and Mudd which cometh out of the Ditches when fcour'd and clean-fed. That which much contributes to the *richnefs* of fuch Mudd and Earth, is the goodnefs of the Hedges, which are tall and thick, and therefore fhed their Leaves plen-tifully in *Autumn*, which mixing and rotting with the Earth, makes it fo *fat* and *ferviceable* in Vegetation. It is moreover a good way to mix this *Ditch - Earth* with fome Dung, which much improves and mollifies it, efpe-cially after it hath lain fome time in heaps. And yet if a fufficient quantity of this *Ditch-Earth* enrich'd with Leaves cannot be got, 'tis a good way to mix *any* fort of Earth with Dung, that it may be fit for ufe and *rot* the fooner, by laying it on heaps.

XI. **When Rye** is cheap and plentiful, (*i. e.* at Two fhillings a Bufhel, or under) it has been found *richly* to anfwer the *Intereft* of the Farmer, to fat his *Oxen* with it after it is ground, tho' not too fmall. The beft time for this practice is in Winter and Spring, when *Beef* fells dear; and the Ufe of it is confirm'd with more reafon ftill, if Hay

happens

happens to be scarce. This, with many other Curiosities in Husbandry, I learnt from Mr. *John Allen*, that ingenious and *faithful* Steward to his Grace the Duke of *Kent*, who hath practis'd it with good Success, and sent the Oxen to *London* for the KING's Table, where the *Beef* was not a little admir'd for its *delicious* taste.

To what has been said before, it may be very proper to add, that forasmuch as Ox-Teams are found best and most profitable, and that a constant succession of fat and lean Cattle is absolutely necessary, every Farmer that keeps Ox-Teams (especially if he buys *the long-Legg'd nimble sort* out of *Huntington-shire*) should rear two Oxen and two Cow-Calves every year, to uphold and preserve his Stock; it being a known Maxim in good Husbandry, That every Farmer, who intends to *thrive*, should always be a *Seller* rather than a *Buyer*.

XII. 𝕲𝖔𝖔𝖉 𝕳𝖚𝖘𝖇𝖆𝖓𝖉𝖗𝖞 requires every Farmer to keep his *Fallows* regular, and in good order, not suffering the Plough to enter (especially the first time) *too deep* ; and not to let the Land want the due number of *Tilts*, viz. four times for *Wheat*, and five for *Barley* : But, above all, that he take care to keep his *Fallows* as clean as possible from *Weeds*, which spoil and *eat out* the strength of his Land and Labour. A great means of preventing this Damage is, (as hath been before hinted) ever to stir the Land in *dry* weather, and upon no account to suffer his Team to go out on that work in a *rainy* Day, it being a certain Truth, that *it is better to do nothing, than nothing to the purpose*. The Custom practis'd in most of the Southern Parts, of confining and folding the *Sheep* by proper Hurdles on the Fallows, should every where be encourag'd, because nothing is more

pro-

proper and natural to all hard Corn than the Dung and Urine of *Sheep*; and the *sooner* such Lands are plow'd after folding, the better, that the Sun *exhale* not too much of its *vertue* and *riches*.

XIII. **Moſt Farmers** are now convinc'd, that ſteeping their Seed-corn (*Wheat* eſpecially) in a ſtrong Brine or Sea-water, and taking away the light Corn, that ſwims at the top, is neceſſary to prevent the Smut ; but becauſe this is often done ſo imperfectly, either ſometimes by only ſprinkling it, or only juſt putting it in, and taking it preſently out again, I think it proper to adviſe the letting the Corn be ſteep'd therein at the leaſt 24 hours, not forgetting (after the Corn is taken out) to ſprinkle unſlaked *Lime* upon it, the better to ſeparate the Corn ; for nothing leſs will entirely prevent the diſeaſe ſo fatal to ſome Grounds and ſome Farmers. Neither ſhould they forget to change their *Seed,* and to chuſe ſuch as grew on a Soil as different as poſſible from that intended to be ſown : However a *Change* is neceſſary, it being a *Maxim* in Husbandry, That all Grain *degenerates* by being *ſown* too long on the ſame Land, or on the ſame ſort of Land.

XIV. **Becauſe** 'tis greatly the Farmer's buſineſs and *Intereſt* to contrive all *honeſt* ways of *improving* every Article, ſo as to anſwer his Labour and Care, it may not be amiſs to put the induſtrious in mind and method of making the beſt of his Stock in two particular *Articles,* much neglected in the North Parts of *England,* and thoſe are *Veal* and *Lamb.* *York, Durham,* and *Newcaſtle* are places *known* to be not only *rich,* but exceeding populous ; to which alſo reſort a vaſt concourſe of Nobility, Gentry, and others, at all public times

of

of Affizes, Seffions, Elections, Horfe-races, &c. And, to make fuch places more frequented by the *Gay* part of Mankind, they have (as in the South) the Contrivances of Plays, Affemblies, and Mufic-meetings : All which call for a *conftant Demand* of every thing eatable which is good in its kind ; and an *encouraging* price would be given by thofe who love to live *elegantly*. Accordingly tho' late years have fhewn a confiderable *Improvement* in the two Articles above, yet an inftructive method of managing thefe two Particulars muft needs be acceptable to the Farmer. As to the firft, it may be obferv'd,

That the Myftery of having good *Veal* lyeth in making it *fat, white*, and *well-tafted*. The laft Quality is often wanted, even when the two former prevail ; which is plainly owing to a too frequent and *over-bleeding*. To obtain therefore *all of them*, no better nor more certain method can be had, than what I obtain'd from a near Relation, who, for the good of the Public, has given me leave to infert it : Let the Calf be laid dry, on *clean Straw* every day laid upon the old, and coop'd up in a little room, but not too ftifling where the Sun comes : His Bed fhould be rais'd a foot from the Ground, hollow'd with Hurdles, fo that the Urine may quickly pafs away, at the fame time taking care that the Calf may not come at the Wall or Ground, to lick it, as he greedily will if not prevented ; inftead of which, a Chalk-ftone fhould be hung up in a String, to encourage his licking *that*, for it will add to the beauty of the Veal. Thus far the Practice is pretty well *known* ; what follows is not fo : For it is a great miftake to let the Calf for the firft fortnight *fuck* as much as he will ; juft to keep him *alive* and *well*, is enough ; and after that, let him blood, and encreafe his *quantum* till he is three weeks old, when you are to dofe

him

him with a 𝕻ill Night and Morning made up only of *Aniseed-water* and the powder of *Chalk*; the *Pill* should be about as big and as long as a Man's Thumb, made up to the consistency of *Paste*, at the same time 'tis used, for otherwise 'twill be dry and hard. The reason of the Prescription is founded on this; That if the Calf is *laxative*, he never will thrive or be fat, and therefore all Art should be used to make him *costive*; and this End is effectually obtain'd by this Composition: And tho' it something abates his appetite to the Milk, yet he will notwithstanding grow very fat the last fortnight, during the time of his *Pills*; for it is not profit to keep a Calf above five or six weeks at most, altho' the practice about *London* extends further; yet neither is their Veal so *delicate* or *well-tasted* as that which is thus manag'd, the Fat of which is observ'd to be hard and firm, and the Flesh exquisitely white and fine by only *two* bleedings, once as before, and the second a week before he dies.

The method of having fat *Lamb* during the *Winter*, is more known, and less difficult: The chief of what I would say upon this Head is, to *perswade* the Farmers in the North to get more into the *Dorsetshire* and *Wiltshire* breed of Sheep, and to provide *all* Conveniencies for housing them, and keeping them clean and sweet; because, as I have observ'd before, there will be a *constant* Demand for such Rarities, and an encouraging price will not be deny'd. Oats, Turnips, and Bran shou'd be the chief Foods of the Ewes during the time of their giving Milk; of which if the Lambs have but enough, and are kept clean and warm, in *little Penns*, they will soon be very fat, and turn to great Profit; as may be guess'd by the ordinary Price given; 15 *s.* for

a fat

a fat Lamb at Five weeks old, and 20 *s.* for a Calf of the same age; but near *London* the Prices are greater.

XV. **Where Dungs**, Compoſts, and moſt of the ſeveral ſorts of Manures are ſcarce or wanting, there is an **Art** to be learnt of *improving poor Land*, or rather of making poor Land *improve it ſelf*, without **Super=inductions:** And this is an Art that ſhould be highly regarded and minded by thoſe who want *theſe Helps*, and would deſire to grow *wiſer* and *richer*. Of this *ſeveral* Hints have been already given; but the whole Myſtery, in ſhort, lieth in ſowing ſuch *Seeds* upon *poor* or *worn-out Land*, that by *plowing-in* the Crop at *Midſummer*, or by *eating* it with a number of *Sheep*, it will receive *Riches* ſufficient to anſwer the Husbandman's Hopes in Tillage, without the *Charge* and *Trouble* of fetching Dung from diſtant places.

Clover, Vetches, Peaſe, Lintels, Buck=wheat, and **Turnips,** are all known to anſwer the purpoſe *here* ſpoken of; and therefore the ſowing of them according to the *improv'd* Practice of the South Parts, ſhould be more *encourag'd* and *practis'd*.

I am well aware that this method of *improving* the poorer ſort of Land hath been the Occaſion of the Complaints of ſome, and of lowering the price of the *richeſt* and *beſt Land*, as it muſt in *reaſon* and of *conſequence* be expected to do. But this is no *juſt* or *real* Objection to the Practice, as it relates either to the public or private; for if the whole Iſland was *all* made rich by *Induſtry* and *Improvements*, the Nation in *general* would be richer too by the quantity of its Products, and their Conſumption in Trade: And as to *private Perſons*, 'tis ſeldom known but that the *poorer Land*

D d d has

has its fhare in moft *confiderable Eftates*, and then the Advantages made will more than over-balance the finking Rent of the beft Land.

To encourage therefore the great Improvements which are to be made by the feveral forts of *artificial Grafs-feeds*, I have thought fit to fubjoyn a *fhort* (but *particular*) Account of them, fhewing the Quantity to be fow'd on an Acre; the Soil they like; the Time of fowing; the ufual Produce, and the Price of *Seed* in L O N D O N.

XVI. Clober.

This is the *richeft* and *beft* of Graffes, 11 pounds will fow an Acre.

Delights in a Soil that is rather *dry* and *warm*, than moift and cold.

To be fow'd ✱ alone at *Michaelmas*, but moft ufually with *Oats* or *Barley* in the Spring.

The Hay to be mow'd the middle of *May*, when it begins to knot.

The produce of Seed from an Acre, two Bufhels.

The Price about 5 *d. per* pound in L O N D O N.

Will laft about three years.

✱ The moft experienc'd Farmers of late years find, that fowing thefe Artificial Grafs-feeds *alone* at *Michaelmas*, anfwers *much* the beft, becaufe the dropping of the Wet from *Oats*, *Barley*, &c. doth not a little leffen the Crop of thefe Artificial Graffes when they are fown together.

Rye=

Rye=grafs.

Three Bufhels and an half fow an Acre; but, if mixt with *Clover*, (which is generally thought beft) eight Pounds of *Clover* with one Bufhel of *Rye-grafs*.

It will grow on any cold, fowre, clayey, weeping Land.

It will laft about Seven Years.

The common Produce of *Seed* from an Acre is about 30 Bufhels. And of Hay two or three Loads.

The middle Price of the *Seed* is 2 *s*. 6 *d*. a Bufhel.

Saint=foyn.

Four Bufhels fow an Acre.

Delights chiefly in a fhallow Ground, or Soil upon a *Lime-ftone*, *Rock*, or *Chalk*.

It will laft about twenty Years; and if Soot is fpread upon the Land at the end of twenty Years, 'twill laft twenty Years more, or longer.

The greateft *Improver* of barren Land of all others.

To be fown alone about *Michaelmas*.

To

To be mow'd for * Hay about the middle of *May* following, when it begins to flower.

The beſt Hay for hard-working Horſes, and commonly produces about 3 or 4 Load from an Acre.

Its Produce of Seed, when ſuffer'd to ſtand till *Midſummer*, is 20 or 25 Buſhels from an Acre.

The Price about Three Shillings *per* Buſhel.

La Lucerne.

Fourteen pounds ſows an Acre on warm Land, in the Spring.

To be mow'd twice a year, *viz.* the beginning of *May*, and again at *Midſummer*.

It is excellent Hay for Horſes, but will not make *any* Cattle fat in ten or twelve Days, as *Mortimer* ſaith.

One Acre will keep three Horſes all the Year.

It will laſt Twenty Years at leaſt.

---

* This Graſs in particular ſhould be mow'd the firſt and ſecond year, becauſe the treading of it with large Cattle, and their being provok'd by the ſweetneſs of it to bite too near the Ground, whilſt the Roots are young and tender, is a great Injury to it, eſpecially in wet weather. *Note,* The Ground whereon this Graſs-ſeed is ſown ſuffers the leaſt of any by conſtant mowing.

Uetches, Lentils, Tares, *and* Buck-Wheat.

These are all profitable Grains, and great *Improvers* of Land, even after the Crop is reap'd; but much more so, if plow'd in when they are in *blossom*.

They require but an ordinary Ground, light Sand, or mellow.

Vetches are of two forts; one will bear the Winter, and should be sown in *November*, and the other in the Spring.

Lentils and *Tares* are vast Encreasers, the Straw of which is one of the sweetest Fodders, especially for young Cattle, and the Seed peculiarly good for Pigeons.

One Bushel of the 'foregoing Grains sows an Acre.

The Produce of which is ordinarily six Bushels.

The middle Price about 4 s. a Bushel.

Buck-wheat, one Bushel sows an Acre; the Encrease is very great, yielding commonly about 50 Bushels upon an Acre: 'Tis an excellent Feed for *Hogs*, *Poultry*, &c. and will grow upon any * dry barren Land.

The time of sowing it is, the latter end of *February*, or beginning of *May*.

The common Price is about 1 s. 6 d. *per* Bushel.

---

* A Bushel of *Buck-wheat* being sow'd upon an Acre of dry barren Land, that has been *worn out* by *over plowing*, the Crop of which being plow'd in about *Midsummer*, when 'tis in its full *pride* and *blossom*, will prove as good a Manuring as Twenty Load of Dung upon an Acre.

E e e   XVII. Tur=

XVII. Turnips.

Becaufe the **Turnip** hath of late years been found to be a very confiderable *Improver* of Land, and brings great *Profit* to the Farmer, fown in large quantities, I rank it among the *improving Grafs-feeds*, and recommend the Ufe of it to all fuch as are not *afham'd* to grow *wifer than their Forefathers*, and will not be difcourag'd from *Experiments*, the fuccefs whereof have been founded on *Reafon* and long *Experience*. There are three forts of *Turnips*, the *round*, the *yellow*, and the *long*, which requires the deeper Soil : They may be fown from *Midfummer* to *Lammas*, or later ; and the Land where they are fown fhou'd be fallow'd twice, and made as *fine* as may be with the Harrow : And when the *Seed* is fown, it fhou'd be harrow'd in with Thorns on the back of the Harrow. After they appear with four Leaves, there will be a neceffity of making ufe of the * Hough, which muft not be neglected, tho' it be too often thought *unneceffary*, for without thinning and forting them they will never *bottom* well ; and yet the *bottoms* are more profitable to Cattle than the *tops*.

If the Land be *over-poor*, the *Turnips* are fubject to be eaten by a *black Fly* ; a fprinkling therefore of rotten Dung (or Soot rather, where it can be got conveniently) on the *top* before they are harrow'd, is very advifeable. Before or

---

* Turnips, when hough'd, ought to be 12 or 13 Inches afunder.

after a Showre is the beſt time for Sowing; but if the firſt or ſecond Sowing miſcarry, (*for miſcarry they often will*) be not diſcourag'd, the *Seed* is very cheap, and the *Labour* not much (being but 4 *d.* a pound, and two pounds ſows an Acre). The Practice of giving the *Turnips* to Cattle in the Houſe ſhou'd not be encourag'd, for that is *robbing* the Land inſtead of *improving* it. The moſt approv'd Method is, to reſerve them for *Winter* feed; and then the *Sheep* (for they are the propereſt Cattle to eat them) ſhou'd be confin'd by Hurdles to an Acre at a time, till the *whole* be well eaten over; and then 'twill be quickly obſerv'd that the *Dung* and *Urine* of the *Sheep*, together with the *rotted* remains of the *Turnips*, will have ſo mellow'd and *enrich'd* the Land, as to make it a fit Recipient for *Barley* in the Spring, and for a Crop of *Beans* or *Peaſe* the following Year, alſo for a Crop of *Wheat* the third, after a Summer-fallow, without other *Helps*. Theſe Crops are wonderfully uſeful to the perfecting the *Winter-Lamb*, by furniſhing the *Ewes* with plenty of Milk.

It may not be amiſs here to inſtruct the Farmer, that a dext'rous Artiſt ſhould provide a Hough ſix or ſeven Inches wide, to determine nearly the diſtance of the Plants after they have gotten four Leaves; for by fixing his Eye upon *One* only at a time, he proceeds in a regular method, and clears his way. Four Men, at 12 *d.* a Day each, will in one Day finiſh an Acre.

The ſame Care that a Farmer takes to make his Land as *fine* as poſſible for *Turnips*, ſhould alſo be obſerv'd with reſpect to *artificial Graſs-ſeeds* above-mention'd; endeavouring to *free* the Land as much as poſſible from all manner of *Trumpery*, ſuch as Stones, Bryars, &c. The want of this Care, and a neglect in **Rolling** the Lands after ſowing,
have

have been the occasion of great Failures in the Crops, to the great discouragement of an *improvable Practice :* For 'tis to be consider'd, that these *Seeds* are small, and if the Mould is not bound *close* to them, they will spend themselves, without being ever able to come forth out of the *Cavities* where they lie.

'Tis to be observ'd, that the Farmers in some parts of the *North* are not yet become so dext'rous in sowing these ✱ *Turnip-seeds* and *Grass-seeds* as they are in the *South,* where constant Practice makes it more familiar, they taking a little betwixt their two Fingers and the Thumb. Till therefore this *Dexterity* can be obtain'd, 'tis advisable to mix the *Seeds* with a convenient quantity of fine *Sand* or *Dust,* the better to fill the *Hand,* in order to sow it with Exactness. But it shou'd be remember'd also, that it is not wisdom to sow these *small Seeds,* except in a *still* Day.

The Farmers in the *North* have got a Notion, that these *artificial Grass-seeds* very much *impoverish* the Land, and therefore are discourag'd from sowing them in any great quantities : But this Discouragement arises from a *mistaken* Practice of constant and *over-much* mowing the Crop, which is indeed the ready way to *beggar* the Land ; as indeed the very same Practice of *over-mowing* beggars the Meadows and Uplands where these *Seeds* are not sown ; it being *now* a

---

* A pound of *Turnip-seed* sown (after Harvest) upon an Acre of light, sandy, or gravelly Land, that has been *worn out by over-plowing,* the Crop of which (*i. e.* the Leaves as well as Roots) being *plow'd in,* will (in about *two* months after) die away and rot, and *strangely* enrich the Land, and prove as good a Manuring as 25 load of Dung upon an Acre. This Method of Husbandry has been practis'd with great Success by that ingenious Gentleman Mr. *Tho. Smith,* at *Eashing* in the Parish of *Godliman* in *Surry.*

known

known *Maxim* among good Husbandmen, and founded on Experience, " That too often and too long *mowing*, is as " great a prejudice to them, as too often and too long *plow-* " *ing* is to Tillage.

I would therefore *perfwade* every Farmer, for the fake of his own *Interest*, to propagate thefe *Grafs-feeds* in a regular method, by fometimes *Summer-eating*, as well as *mowing* the fame ; not forgetting fometimes alfo to *plow in* a full Crop, when 'tis in its full *pride* and *bloffom* ; and he will quickly find the great Advantage thereof in the *richnefs* of the Land, nay, in feeing the Land 𝕰𝖓𝖗𝖎𝖈𝖍 𝖎𝖙 𝖘𝖊𝖑𝖋. And this method (as I have already obferv'd) is fingularly profitable and ufeful, where *Dung* and *Compofts* are not eafily obtain'd, or are to be fetch'd at a great diftance.

F f f AN

AN

ABSTRACT;

Or, A short Collection of the several sorts of

𝕯𝖚𝖓𝖌𝖘 𝖆𝖓𝖉 𝕮𝖔𝖒𝖕𝖔𝖘𝖙𝖘;

Together with

All *other Manures for the Improvement of the seve-*
ral sorts of Land, as practis'd in most Counties
in England; *being of ready Use to* every Far-
mer, by seeing in a little compass their several
Natures and Properties.

XVIII. **Horse** and **Cow-Dung**, &c. being mixt with
Ditch-Earth where the Leaves of thick Hedges
rot, or being mixt with the Mudd of Ponds, or (for want of the
said rich *Ditch-earth* or *Mudd*) you may mix any sort of Earth
with the said Dungs, and it will cause it to rot *much* sooner,
and will prove an *admirable* Manure for most sorts of Arable
or Pasture Land. This method is practis'd very much in *Es-*
sex,

fex, where they lay it in great heaps, in a wafte place nigh where 'tis intended to be fpent. The quantity of this *Compoft* for Clay-land is about 2 0 Loads upon an Acre ; but the red *Hazely* Brick-earth, or light Sands, will not require above 1 0 or 1 5 Loads upon an Acre, becaufe it muft be renew'd oftner than the Clay-lands.

Sheeps=Dung for cold-tillage Clay-lands is the *beft* of *all* Dungs ; and becaufe it cannot fo conveniently be gather'd together as other Dungs, 'tis commonly convey'd upon the faid Lands by folding the *Sheep* upon it, penn'd up together a-Nights by proper Hurdles, by which means both *Dung* and *Urine* are fpent upon the Land. I have feen good *Improvements* in *Effex* by this Dung, where they fold the *Sheep* in cover'd Folds, and mix their Dung with *Ditch-earth, Mudd,* &c. as aforemention'd, which caufes the Dung to fpread *much further.* Likewife in the *Weftern* parts of *England* (becaufe of the *Excellency* of this Dung *above all others*) they houfe their *Sheep* a-Nights, and litter them with clean Straw. This is found by *late Experience* the beft Manuring, and *well anfwers* the trouble.

Hogs=Dung (next to *Sheeps-Dung*) is the richeft and fatteft of any, both for *Tillage* and *Pafture*, efpecially the latter : One Load of this will go as far two of others. It may likewife be mixt as above, to make it go the further.

Humane Ordure, for hot, dry, burning Lands, makes a *great Improvement*. To make it commodious for carriage, 'tis often mixt with other Dungs or *Ditch-earth*, &c. as aforemention'd, and is us'd very much in *Kent*, &c. with good fuccefs, efpecially for Pafture Land.

Pigeons=

𝕻𝖎𝖌𝖊𝖔𝖓𝖘=𝕯𝖚𝖓𝖌 being of a very *hot* nature, and *full* of Salts, agrees beſt when laid on *cold* Lands, either *Tillage*, *Paſture*, or *Meadow*. When uſed for *Tillage*, it ſhou'd be ſown by hand *after* the Grain is ſow'd, and in the ſame manner : About 30 Buſhels will ſow an Acre. It anſwers for one Year only, but produces a great Crop, even on the moſt *barren* Land, if the Year prove any thing dripping.

𝕳𝖊𝖓𝖘=𝕯𝖚𝖓𝖌, and the Dungs of other Poultry, are *all* very *good*, and full of *Nitre*, tho' none of them ſo rich as *Pigeon-dung*. Becauſe of its hanging together, 'tis more difficult to ſow than *Pigeons-dung*; therefore 'tis beſt mixing it with other Dungs, or with *Aſhes*, *Earth*, or *Sand*.

𝕾𝖊𝖆=𝖈𝖔𝖆𝖑=𝕬𝖘𝖍𝖊𝖘, for cold Meadow and Paſture Land, is an *admirable Improver*, cauſing the Soil to run much to *wild Trefoil* and *wild Clover*, (which of all others is the *ſweeteſt* and *richeſt* Feed for Cattle) and in ſuch *abundance* too, that it will keep a double number of Stock. 'Tis alſo a very laſting Manure, eſpecially if you have the opportunity to lay 20 or 25 Loads upon an Acre; tho' much leſs will anſwer very well. This Manure is not ſo proper for *Tillage* as for *Paſture*.

𝕾𝖔𝖆𝖕=𝕬𝖘𝖍𝖊𝖘 (after the *Soap-boilers* have done with them) is an excellent Manure for both *Tillage* and *Paſture*; about 8 or 9 Loads will manure an Acre, and tends to the deſtroying of *Furze*, *Broom*, and *Fern*, if apply'd after grubbing at Midſummer. This Manure will laſt four or five Crops.

𝕻𝖔𝖙=𝕬𝖘𝖍𝖊𝖘 is a very good Manure for moſt ſorts of *Paſture* Grounds; but becauſe the wet is left in them by the *Pot-men*, which

which has caufed the Lee to draw out good part of the Salts, therefore a *greater* quantity muft be laid on the Land than the aforefaid *Soap-Afhes.*

Soot is an Extraordinary Manure for both Tillage and Pafture-Land, efpecially if it be Soot from *Sea-Coal,* becaufe 'tis much the ftrongeft, and fulleft of *Nitre,* and anfwers beft upon *cold Clays,* when about Forty Bufhels is laid upon an Acre; which will likewife be a means of deftroying *Weeds* and other *Trumpery.* If once in four or five years you fow your Land whereon *Saint-foyn* has been fown with this Manure, 'twill very much encreafe the Crop, and make it laft feveral Years longer.

Malt-Duft is another confiderable *Improver* of Land, which muft be fow'd by hand, as they do the *Seed :* It will give a ftrange *Life* and *Encreafe* to a Crop of *Barley,* efpecially after a fhowre of Rain : 'Tis near as ftrong as *Pigeons-dung,* and fhou'd be ufed in the fame manner, by fowing about Forty Bufhels upon an Acre; but you are not to expect more from it than the advantage of one Crop.

Rags of all forts, both *Linnen, Woollen,* and *Leather,* make a very great *Improvement* on chalky binding tillage Land, *vaft quantities* of them being fetch'd from *London* to *Dunftable* and other Parts where chalky Hills are, only to lay on their *Lands,* where they chop them very fmall, and ftrew them juft after the fowing of the Corn, allowing 24 Bufhels to an Acre. Shreads of Leather, old Shoes, Hats, or Stockings, as they are longer rotting and decaying, fo they *laft* the longer.

Wheat

𝕎𝕖𝕒𝕣, a Sea-weed growing chiefly on such Rocks as are cover'd only at High-water, is good to be laid on *Tillage* for one Crop, the drying and burning of which makes *Kilp*, used in making Glass. This *Kilp* also being *steept* in water, is used to *dilute* the *Allom Liquor*. After the *Allom-makers* have done with it, 'tis laid upon the Land; and altho' a great quantity of the *Nitrous Particles* are drawn from it, yet nevertheless 'tis an *admirable Manure* both for Tillage and Pasture Lands, and has made *great Improvements* round *Sands-end* in *Yorkshire*, where the chief *Allom-works* of His Grace the Duke of BUCKINGHAM are. The common Allowance for either *Meadow* or *Pasture* is about six Loads upon an Acre. These Ashes soon dissolve, so will not last above four or five Crops of Tillage; but much longer, and are accounted much better, for *Pasture* and *Meadow*, than *Tillage*.

𝕃𝕚𝕞𝕖, of *all* other Manures, has (of late years) made the *Greatest Improvement*, both of *Tillage* and *Pasture*, so that the *Industrious Farmer* thinks almost no Pains or Cost too much to procure it. It agrees with *all* sorts of Soils, except the two Extreams of a *dusty* Sand and the *strongest* Clays. It *improves* all light Soils, by adding *Tenacity* to them : Likewise all *heathy* and *moory* Grounds over-run with *Furze, Brakes, Broom*, &c. when turn'd up by the Plough, are *surprizingly* benefited by it, insomuch that many Lands, suppos'd not worth above Two shillings an Acre, are in the North of *England* made worth above Fifteen shillings an Acre, by vertue of this Noble Manure of 𝕃𝕚𝕞𝕖 ; about Eighty or Ninety Bushels of which being laid upon an Acre in Tillage, will last five or six years.

𝕮𝖍𝖆𝖑𝖐,

Chalk, one Load of which should be mixt with two Loads of Dung or other rich Earth : According to this proportion, if you lay a good quantity in a heap to *ferment* and *incorporate*, 'tis an admirable Manure for all cold soure, and also gravelly Land, and will produce incredible Crops of *Corn* for several years together, by laying about Twenty Loads upon an Acre. And when the time of Tillage is expir'd, in order to lay down the same for Grass, lay on Twenty Loads of *Chalk* alone upon an Acre, and it will perform wonders.

Marle is of several sorts; the *best* is pure and unmixt, and will dissolve in *Water* : 'Tis an *excellent* Manure to fix light Sands, but it has been disputed whether it has any *fertilizing* Quality of it self, because it doth not send forth the *first Year.* The common quantity in *Staffordshire* is Three hundred Loads upon an Acre, which will last without marling again above Twenty Years, if kept in Tillage and Pasture *interchangeably,* which is most advisable : And you ought to give the Land a sprinkling of Dung for every Crop of *Wheat* you reap; for this will keep the Land in a perfect *state of Health,* and help to loosen the binding Quality of the *Marle.*

It should not be forgot, that the *Bottoms* and *Scourings of Ponds* (especially such as are surrounded with Hedges and Trees) are *excellent* for *all sorts* of Soils, to be laid upon the surface of *Meadows* and *Pastures* in *Autumn, Winter,* or *Spring;* but the two first Seasons are the best. The Leaves of Trees in process of time do much *impregnate* the Mudd with *Salts,* and therefore the *older* the *Ponds* are before they are scoured, the

the better. If the Meadow or Pasture be cover'd over pretty thick with it, as they ought, it will last many Years, and produce abundance of *Trefoil*.

Some late Experience hath discover'd, that even the *black moorish* Soil taken off the *Fells*, which would not be perswaded to bear or produce any thing but an unprofitable *Ling*, if 'tis laid together with *Lime*, and *Litter* or *long Dung* from the Stable, in equal quantities, for a Year, 'twill make vast Improvements on Meadow-ground, laid on in the Spring : The *Lime* and *Dung* both tend to *ferment* and *rot* the Soil, and at the same time give such *Tenacity* to it, that it soon becomes *mellow* and *rich*, and fit to answer the Expectations of a diligent Lover of *Improvements*.

𝔖𝔢𝔞=𝔩𝔞𝔫𝔡, to those who live within a mile or two of the Sea, and have any stiff clayey Land to lay it on, is a most *excellent* Manure, especially if it be taken *wet*, just after the Tide has left it ; and the more of it, the better. The reason of its giving such *Fertility* to Land of a clayey nature is two-fold ; *first*, because it tends to separate the Parts of Clay, which otherwise would retain *stagnating Water*, and thereby *Starve* and *Chill* all infant Plants : And, *secondly*, because being mixt with Salt, it gives much the same *Riches* as are expected from Dung fill'd with *Nitre* and *Salt*. The same is to be said with respect to *Sea-shells* and the *Bones and Refuse of Fish*, all which are afforded in *great* quantities near the Fishing-Towns on His Grace the Duke of *Buckingham's* Estates in *York-shire*.

A N

A N

ABSTRACT

Of the feveral Sorts of

Earths and Soils

On which the proper Dungs and Ma-
nures are directed to be laid, agreeable to their
feveral Natures.

XIX. **S A N D,** which of all others wants generally
moft Help and Improvement, and is in its na-
ture loofe and porous, quickly lofing the fattening Moifture
that falls from the Heavens, is beft and moft rationally
mended by all fuch Dungs as give *Tenacity* and a holding
Nature to it : And fuch are the Dungs taken from *Cows* and
Hogs, which are cold and binding. There is indeed much
difference in the Nature of *Sands* ; fome are *cold*, and others
hot ; fome are *rich*, and others *poor* ; but all of them want
fomething to hold their Parts together, which is beft done,
as is before faid, by the Dung of *Cows*, *Oxen*, or *Hogs*.

H h h

Much

Much the same is to be said of *Gravel*, especially when it is not mixt with *Clay*, *Chalk*, or *Loam*; there all holding and binding Dungs are most proper, *Humane Ordure* not excepted, and *Rags* included.

There are also other light Soils, that are not properly either Sand or Gravel, which must be mended with the aforesaid Dungs, and these are light *chiselly Soils*, lying on the top of scaley Rocks of *Free* or *Lime-Stone*, and are of consequence mixt with many small Stones, which turn up with the Plow. Besides the aforesaid *holding* Dungs, these Soils are also properly mended with *Chalk*, *Clay*, *Marle*, or the *Bottoms of Ponds* : But if these Soils (as commonly they do) prove shallow upon the Rock, the best way to improve and enrich them is, to lay them down with *Saint-foyn*.

Clay, when 'tis pretty much unmixt, is the other Extream to what went before, and must have different Manures for its Tillage, such as *Horse-dung, Sea-coal Ashes, Sea-sand, Drift-sand, Pigeon* and *Hen-dung*, and the *Bottoms of Wood-yards*, and all little enough to mellow and loosen the Parts of some untractable *Clays*.

Chalk has most of the Properties of *Clay*, especially that of holding the Water, and wanting something to loosen its Parts, tho' it is generally of a warmer nature : Accordingly all the Dungs named under the last Article (as also *Rags*) improve and mend it. And when so mended, 'tis observ'd to bear the *best* and the *finest Wheat*.

Loam, properly so call'd, is that Soil which partakes of a due mixture of both *Clay* and *Sand*, having all the *good*
Pro-

Properties of *both*, and none of the *bad* ones; and is generally of such a sufficient depth, that it bears all sorts of *Vegetables* to perfection, both Trees, Plants, and Grain. Accordingly 'tis to be remark'd, that just so far as the *Clay* on the
one hand, or the *Sand* on the other, are observ'd to prevail
and to exceed their proportion in these sorts of mixt *Earths*,
so far they are proportionably *worse*, and less useful for Vegetation, in their own Nature: And therefore of consequence
the proper and discreet *Application* of Dungs must be made
accordingly, as directed above. But yet such happy Soils and
mixt Earths, as we call *Loam*, are frequently to be met with;
which therefore must rationally be suppos'd to be mended,
enrich'd, and improv'd (when *worn out*) by a mixture of
all sorts of Manures and Dungs both of a *holding* and *loosening*
nature.

🌸🌸🌸🌸🌸🌸🌸🌸🌸🌸🌸🌸🌸🌸🌸👑🌸🌸🌸🌸🌸🌸🌸🌸🌸🌸🌸🌸🌸🌸🌸

The Conclusion.

XX. **WI**thout entring upon (or attempting) a general
System, but to make this Treatise as useful as
may be, I think it not improper to let the FARMER know
How some general Annoyances to a FARM may be remov'd
without any great Charge.

Whins or **Furze** may easily be destroy'd when they
return or come up again, as soon as the Land is laid down
for Grass after Tillage; for 'tis observ'd, that they are by
Hand easily pluckt up by the Roots after a Frost, when the
Ground

Ground is loofe and tender : This in the *Weft of England* is call'd *Weeding* the Land. Conftant mowing them down while young will do the fame thing.

𝕭𝖗𝖔𝖔𝖒 is eafily deftroy'd by *cutting, chopping,* and afterwards *mowing* it down at 𝕸𝖎𝖉𝖘𝖚𝖒𝖒𝖊𝖗, within two or three Inches of the Ground : After which if it fhould have a *refurrection,* yet the *fecond* Tryal will *effectually* compleat the *Cure.*

𝕽𝖚𝖘𝖍𝖊𝖘 are alfo eafily deftroy'd by *mowing* them down near the Ground at *Spring* and *Midfummer,* not forgetting to lay a good fprinkling of *Lime,* or a good quantity of *Horfe, Pigeon,* or *Hen-dung* at the Roots, and you'll fee no more of them.

𝕱𝖊𝖗𝖓 is more difficult to deftroy than any of the 'foremention'd, becaufe they ftrike fuch a *deep* root into the Earth ; but neverthelefs conftant mowing in *Spring,* and at *Midfummer,* and afterwards laying *Dung* or *Lime* at the Roots, will anfwer the End in deftroying them in a great meafure.

F I N I S.